The History of
Dale Hollow Lake

Darren Shell
Sheryl Shell

Fideli Publishing

Introduction

A Note From Sheryl

When I moved to this lake with its Tennessee and Kentucky shores over two and one-half decades ago, different friends and acquaintances commented that some day the lake and area would lose its beauty for me. Wrong! After all this time, it not only holds that breathtaking beauty but it has now faced me two-fold.

Darren asked me to give him a little "push" to get him motivated on this project, but I believe the tide has turned as he has gotten me enthused. Now, we would like to inspire you.

Come along with Darren to the river days and vast pasture lands of our ancestors and friends we never knew. He will tell his stories and views of what lies beneath these pristine waters of today, and he will let you envision the totally changed environment and surroundings of present day.

Maybe you can compare "then to now" and determine for yourself where the real beauty lies. As you read along, ask yourself if you would rather have been drawn to this area before the lake was formed and endure the hardships of our early settlers or just simply enjoy the Dale Hollow Lake of present and the future it holds for our loved ones? It has been and will always be a remarkable place to remember and visit.

So, with that said, come along with the Gravedigger as he blends present day stories and pictures with their historical past. He will bring forth this great history of yesterday, revive it, and unfold it into the way we see it today.

By compiling this book, I can only hope we can " move" you as much as it has touched both of us. Enjoy.

Thank you, Darren, for the love and encouragement you have shown me. ~

Sheryl Shell
(*The Gravedigger's Mom*)
2008

Authors Darren and Sheryl Shell, April 2008

A Note from Darren

I never wanted to be a historian. I never wanted to be an author. In fact, for years, about all I really wanted out of life was to live and work and play on Dale Hollow Lake. And that, my friends, I have done in multitudes. I work hard, play hard, and love this lake like no other place in this world. I have been to other lakes around the country and have truly enjoyed what they have to offer. But those lakes aren't Dale Hollow. For me, this one is it. And by the grace of God and the love of my family and friends, I have been able to live my life on this wonderful body of water for decades. These shores have changed me—they've sparked my interest down to the minutest of details of age-old history here. I can talk for hours about the old buildings and people, the huge bridges and cemeteries, things that existed here before me. The smallest of artifacts from the old Obey River Valley enthuses me to no end.

And then one day, someone suggested I write some of this stuff down. I then realized that I should have paid much closer attention to my writing classes in school. Sometimes spell-check on my computer can't even recognize the words I try to spell. But thanks to some wonderful proofreaders, I'm able to tell the cool stories that happened way back in yesteryear...right here on the Dale.

A few years ago, I wrote my first Dale Hollow story. I've now compiled numerous books and countless articles in newspapers and different publications around the area. I give tours of the campgrounds, telling history through the fictional eyes of an "old gravedigger" from the lake-building era.

This book is a compilation of my articles and stories from the past couple of years. Some of these stories overlap my other books, just as history overlaps itself in many ways. I hope that through these stories, you can come to love this fantastic reservoir with the same love we have for it. I've been told I have a unique set of eyes. I see the water of the present—and the history of yesterday…and I want to share it all. With my mother's heart-felt help, together we will try to unfurl history and enrichen the present…all right here on Dale Hollow. Having said that, one might think I'm a Momma's-boy. Well, dang-it…we've hiked the trails, swam the shores, crawled the caves, and just about everything this ol' lake has to offer. So if that makes me a Momma's-boy, then I guess I am. And if you don't like it…I'm tellin' Mom. You'll be in serious *TROUBLE!*

Thanks to all of you that have taken time to say such kind words about my (our) stories. Thank you for your interest in my favorite place on earth. 'Cause, this old Gravedigger loves what he does. And even though I never really wanted to be—I think I've become a historian, and maybe even an author…and I guess the rest is history.

I'd like to express my gratitude to those authors that have donated articles to enhance this book. Mr. Mark Willis, Mr. Andy Mitchell of Mitchell Media, Mr. Jesse Walton and mother, Lori of Lake Times News, Terry and Andrea Burkhardt of Dale Hollow Marketing Group, Mr. Thomas Weaver of the Dale Hollow Horizon, Mr. Tom Weir, and also the staff of the Clinton County News—I thank you all for your generous help. My publishers at Fideli have been sweetheart ladies to work with—thanks. I have a couple hundred other people to thank on this project, but I'll do it in person rather than here. That way I can do it with a hug. But to my mother I owe my greatest thanks. This book would not have happened without her great effort and love—and that whole "raising me" thing. She and Dad are the best. I love you both. ~

Best Regards to all,

Darren, The Gravedigger

The History of
Dale Hollow Lake

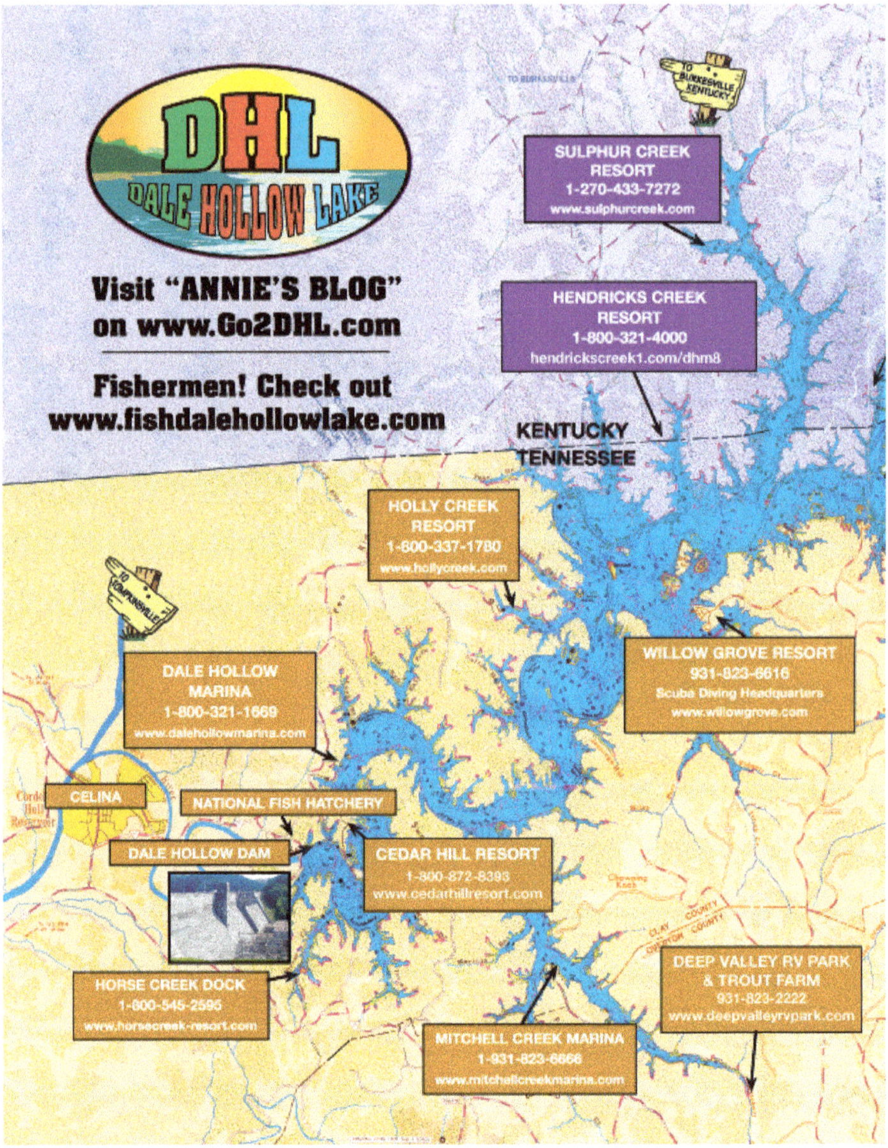
DHL
DALE HOLLOW LAKE
Visit "ANNIE'S BLOG" on www.Go2DHL.com
Fishermen! Check out www.fishdalehollowlake.com
TO BURKESVILLE KENTUCKY
SULPHUR CREEK RESORT
1-270-433-7272
www.sulphurcreek.com
HENDRICKS CREEK RESORT
1-800-321-4000
hendrickscreek1.com/dhm8
KENTUCKY
TENNESSEE
HOLLY CREEK RESORT
1-800-337-1780
www.hollycreek.com
WILLOW GROVE RESORT
931-823-6616
Scuba Diving Headquarters
www.willowgrove.com
DALE HOLLOW MARINA
1-800-321-1669
www.dalehollowmarina.com
CELINA
NATIONAL FISH HATCHERY
DALE HOLLOW DAM
CEDAR HILL RESORT
1-800-872-8393
www.cedarhillresort.com
DEEP VALLEY RV PARK & TROUT FARM
931-823-2222
www.deepvalleyrvpark.com
HORSE CREEK DOCK
1-800-545-2595
www.horsecreek-resort.com
MITCHELL CREEK MARINA
1-931-823-6666
www.mitchellcreekmarina.com

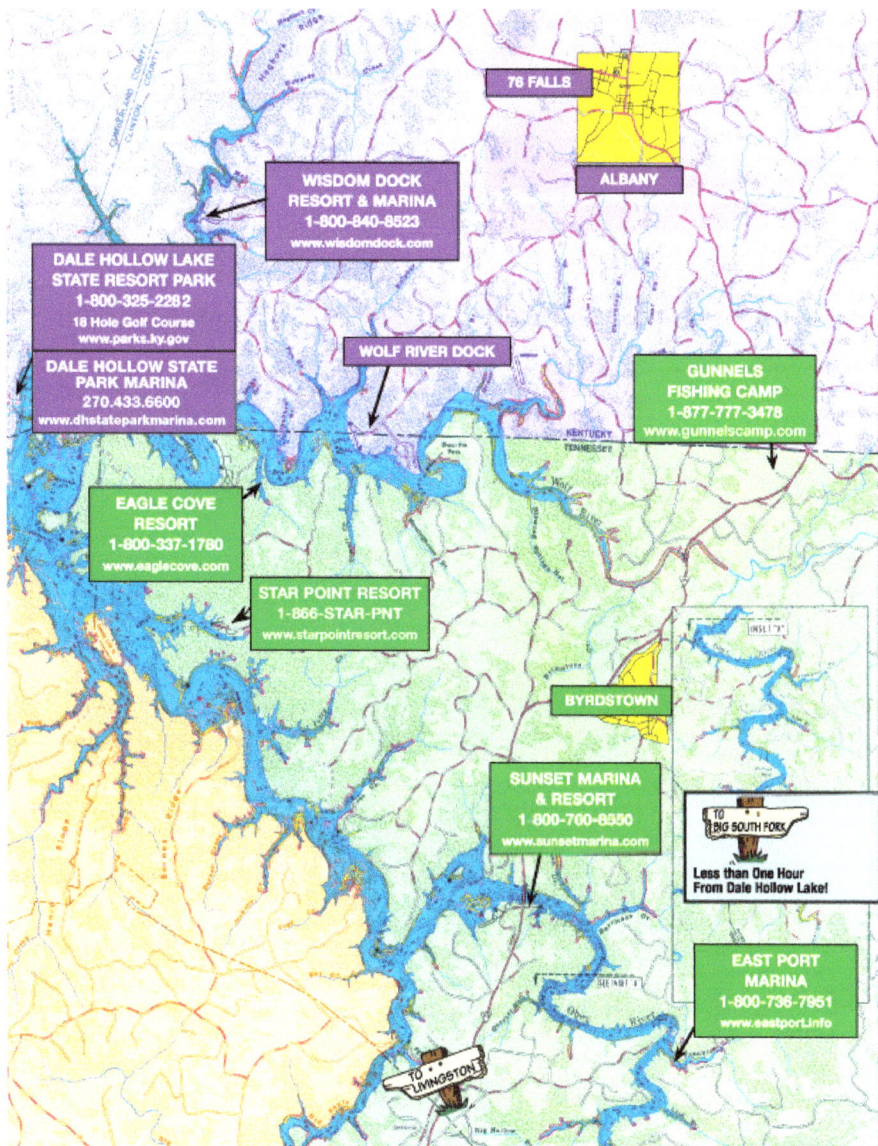

76 FALLS

ALBANY

WISDOM DOCK
RESORT & MARINA
1-800-840-8523
www.wisdomdock.com

DALE HOLLOW LAKE
STATE RESORT PARK
1-800-325-2282
18 Hole Golf Course
www.parks.ky.gov

DALE HOLLOW STATE
PARK MARINA
270.433.6600
www.dhstateparkmarina.com

WOLF RIVER DOCK

GUNNELS
FISHING CAMP
1-877-777-3478
www.gunnelscamp.com

EAGLE COVE
RESORT
1-800-337-1780
www.eaglecove.com

STAR POINT RESORT
1-866-STAR-PNT
www.starpointresort.com

BYRDSTOWN

SUNSET MARINA
& RESORT
1-800-700-8550
www.sunsetmarina.com

TO
BIG SOUTH FORK

Less than One Hour
From Dale Hollow Lake!

EAST PORT
MARINA
1-800-736-7951
www.eastport.info

TO
LIVINGSTON

9

Story Selection

The Dam Project

Dale Hollow Dam
Photo courtesy of U.S. Army Corps of Engineers

We will attempt to give a few important details in regards to the making of the dam. The Morris-Knudsen Company secured the rights to begin evacuating homes and businesses throughout the Obey River Valley in 1941/42. Of course, this evacuation infuriated many of the river folk that never intended to leave the valley of their birth. Some say it was a time of vast sorrow. Others suggest a time of new and exciting change. Regardless of which side of the coin one chooses to adhere, this was a time like few will ever see in this cross-section of modern time. The red tape of present day would negate any such vast plans if such were presented in the arena of modern day America. Right Wings and Left Wings would battle over everything from salamanders to oil wells. And our tax dollars would begin yet another travel down life's long and unexpected road.

That's how the wheels of progress turn. But in 1941, things were quite different. Rather than bore you with the internet details, here's a few cool and worthy photos. Enjoy.

This is the Jason Terry home site in 1942,
in the community known as Holman's Bottom.
This is where the dam now resides.

Transformer Controller Site, March, 1942

Diversion Canal for dam, March, 1942

Dam, August, 1942

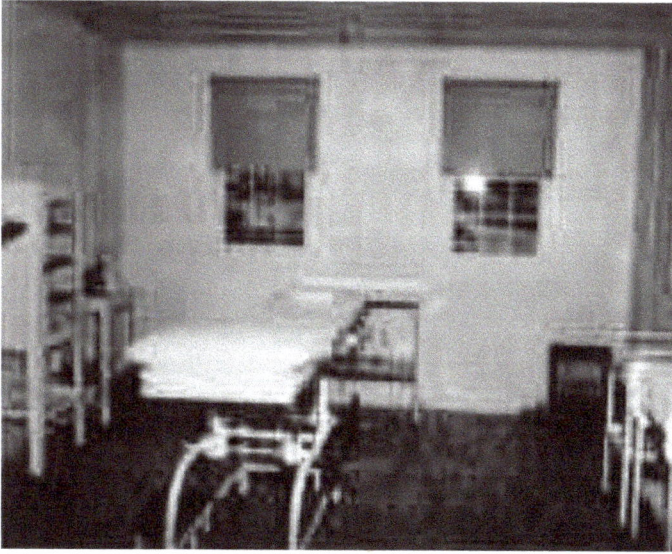

Operating Room, dam site, April, 1942

Hatchery Below Dam and Recreation Area
Visitors Welcome

Dale Hollow Power Plant, 10 June 1947. Fire at Morrison-
Knudsen carpenter shop.   Q3-61/164

Sewell Bend below First Island
Photo courtesy of Mark Willis

Nine men killed during construction of Dale Hollow Dam honored with plaque

By ED CAHILL
Citizen-Statesman Editor

An open house held at the Dale Hollow Dam Power Plant on Sunday, June 10, 2001,featured a dedication ceremony for a plaque listing the names of nine men who were killed during the construction of the dam.

The nine men listed on the plaque are:

* Alex West, who died in a vehicle accident hauling supplies on April 17, 1942.

* Harry Nicholson, who died when he fell to his death on August 26, 1942.

* R.R. Langston, who died while working with heavy equipment on October 2, 1942.

* Ress White, who died in a vehicle accident on his way to work on March 10, 1942.

* Fowler Dulworth, who died in a vehicle accident on his way to work on March 10, 1943.

* Herbert White, who died on March 11, 1943 after being in the same vehicle accident on his way to work on March 10, 1943.

* Boss Hestand, who fell from a raft transporting workers across the river and drowned on May 6, 1943.

* Jack Johnson, who died when trash racks fell on him on July 22, 1943.

* Irvin Roberts, who died when the trash racks fell on him also on July 22, 1943.

Also recognized during the brief ceremony was Arley Hood, who lost his life during the clearing of the lands around Dale Hollow Lake, and the 118 individuals who have lost their lives as a result of drowning in Dale Hollow Lake.

According to Shirley Cherry, administrative assistant to the superintendent of the Dale Hollow Dam Power Plant, the names of the nine men listed on the plaque were gathered from different sources, including newspaper stories, former workers on the dam project and family members.

"If anyone was overlooked, it was due to lack of records or information and we greatly apologize," Cherry said. "We just had to go on the information we had."

The plaque, which is mounted on a post beneath a small shelter, is located near the entrance to the Dale Hollow Dam Power Plant.

Anniversary Poster with Corps Officials' Signatures

Willow Grove,
the Town That Drowned

Not unlike the fabled city of Atlantis, the old town of Willow Grove, Tennessee, is now under a lavish blanket of water. The murky depths of Dale Hollow Lake still house the shadowy foundations of what was once a beautiful and thriving valley town. The winding and crystal clear waters of the Obey River wound through many small communities and towns as it meandered its way toward the Cumberland. Willow Grove sat along the banks of Irons Creek and was lovingly named from the Willow trees that grew along its shores. For its day, this little town was not so little. It had service stations, churches, general stores, and one of the largest school buildings within miles. It even had a large gymnasium, where children rode horse-back to basketball games. A large grist mill sat in the middle of what is now Willow Grove Campground, and it overlooked the bustling Tennessee Highway 53 that cut through the center of town. The clip-clop of hooves echoed through the streets as wagons were drawn by horses and mules, and the chuckles of children scampering through the streets filled the air. The crisp, clean air smelled of freshly cut hay and the wisps of smoke from the fires burning in the kitchen cook stoves. And life was grand.

Willow Grove, late 1930s

And then it happened. The year was 1942. The once cheerful and quaint valley town of Willow Grove was now forlorn and solemn. Aside from the sad sights of the town's men marching off to World War II, the residents faced a horrific and depressing dilemma. The government was forcing the families and friends of this closely-knit community to move away. The United States government was buying their property. It was demolishing their homes and businesses...to build a dam. The farm fields tilled by their forefathers were now dozed clean of fences and barns. The ever incessant sounds of chainsaws hummed day in and day out. Bonfires were kindled in every field and the loud claps of dynamite shook the earth. And the beautiful little valley town of Willow Grove now looked like a war zone.

Despite the anguish in their hearts, the community gathered one last time before the move. On July 18, 1942, the people of Willow Grove united at a town picnic. The Corps of Engineers set it up and made certain that county agents were on hand to help the townspeople with the inevitable move. Amid the anger and sadness, one of the town's most beloved members gave a particularly moving speech. Dr. Edward Clark convinced the people of Willow Grove to press forward and offered hope to those forced to move. His words softened the blow of moving. And for the people of Willow Grove, Father Time pressed on, and the water did rise.

The Last Gathering at the Willow Grove Church of Christ

In the years that followed, the rough terrain around the lake began to take shape. Marinas were built where the old roads entered the lake. Tiny wooden boats dotted the shores and people all over the country were beginning to love this special lake named Dale Hollow, in remembrance of the Dale family that owned the large tract of land that now houses a giant chunk of concrete that holds back billions of gallons of water. Dale Hollow Dam now stands in remembrance of William Dale and the hundreds of his descendents that now populate the surrounding communities.

Willow Grove Reunion, late 1960s

The people of old Willow Grove still get together once a year for a reunion. On Sunday of Labor Day weekend, once again the familiar voices of the townspeople fill the air as memories flow and laughter helps heal the hearts of those that still mourn the loss of their old home town.

THE WILLOW GROVE CROWD was estimated to have climbed near to 700 before the homecoming came to a close. †

Willow Grove Reunion, late 1960s

So, when your feet dangle in the cool, clear water of Dale Hollow, and your face is warmed by the brilliant colors of the setting sun, give a little thank you to the people of old Willow Grove and its surrounding communities. Say a little prayer for those who endured the hardships of this lake's making. And remember in your heart...that these shores contain so very much more than just water. ~

HOME OF DR. CLARK AT RIGHT

From Irons Creek Bridge

Hay and Martin General Merchandise in Willow Grove

Upchurch Esso Station in Willow Grove

Upchurch and Hogan boys at Willow Grove Cash Store
Late 1930s

*Willow Grove County Fair, very early 1900s
It perhaps was the much-advertised 1916 Fair.*

*A gathering of the old Willow Grove Doctors
At the Willow Grove Reunion, late 1940s*

Printed in the Livingston Enterprise 7-31-07

By ANDY MITCHELL
Editor/publisher

Livingston Enterprise Ad from fall of 2007

On a dark and misty night as the moon slowly peaked through the clouds, dozens of people gathered at the Willow Grove Campground to hear master storyteller and author Darren Shell tell tales of the history and lore surrounding the creation of Dale Hollow Lake and the once proud community of Willow Grove.

Like a spider spinning his web, Shell, dressed as a gravedigger, led those brave enough to participate on a ghost tour through the campground last Tuesday evening, spinning tales of heartbreak and sorrow as the people of Willow Grove were relocated during the creation of Dale Hollow Lake. And like the spider, Shell connected each story while he spun his web, as the participants were drawn deep into the stories surrounding Willow Grove.

"This started out as a history tour originally," Shell began as participants gathered at the Willow Grove Campground gatehouse. "But the people with cameras started telling me such neat stuff, it kind of developed into a ghost tour," he said, referring to what some participants had captured on their digital cameras.

"As the tour goes on, I want you to know that all of this is documented fact I tell you about," Shell emphasized. "I can't promise you're going to see ghosts. I don't know that I've actually seen a ghost here, but I've seen some interesting stuff happen.

"A lot of non-believers have come on this, and some have gone away disappointed," Shell paused, "And some of them have run away to their cars."

As tree frogs spoke and crickets chirped, providing an eerie symphony for the event, Shell led the participants on the ghost tour through the campground. He encouraged participants to use their cameras to take pictures in any direction when they felt it necessary, hopefully capturing small, spherical white images known as "orbs," what some people believe to be ghosts in the form of energy.

"When you feel it is when it usually happens," he said, encouraging participants to share with others any orb images they may capture. "I'm not sure what they are, but I know when we find them they seem to be in places where historical things have happened – where history good and bad has happened."

And the spider began to spin his web of tales, starting first with the creation of Dale Hollow Lake.

Orb photo from Willow Grove Park, fall 2007

"Most of you know that Dale Hollow is a man-made lake...part of this campground and beyond was an old city, the biggest city that was covered in water when the lake was made in 1942.

...You don't just pick up and move a city," Shell emphasized. "You move homes, and you move people."

Shell went on to tell the participants the people of Willow Grove were heartbroken when forced to leave their homes, as well as those in other communities that were relocated because of the creation of the lake. Homes were demolished and timber cut during the relocation, including the moving of many graves.

"There were also several cemeteries back that one same road here at this junction (a highway that went through Willow Grove when the lake was created)," Shell told the participants as they began their walk through the dark campground. "They were documented as moved by the Corps of Engineers. The Corps of Engineers moved 106 cemeteries off of Dale Hollow," Shell continued, as one of the participants gasped "Oh my God."

Some of the cemeteries had only a few graves, but many had over 100 graves in them he explained.

"Nobody wanted this job," he emphasized. If you think about it, back in 1942 most of those graves were not the nice, big pretty graves you see now. They were in a rough section of the woods, and probably they've been there for 100 years already and quite possibly there was nothing left to dig if they were going to dig up the grave in the first place.

"If it were fairly damp soil, their old wooden casket would have rotted. Probably their bones might have rotted in that amount of time. The only thing left was just teeth and belt buckles and boots."

He went on to tell the participants you can still see places where the graves were.

"You can go out on the lake right now, and I can tell you where you can step up on shore and see rows of these great big holes where big caskets were moved. But, there were also many, many, many out there that's just got a little divot – that's just about all."

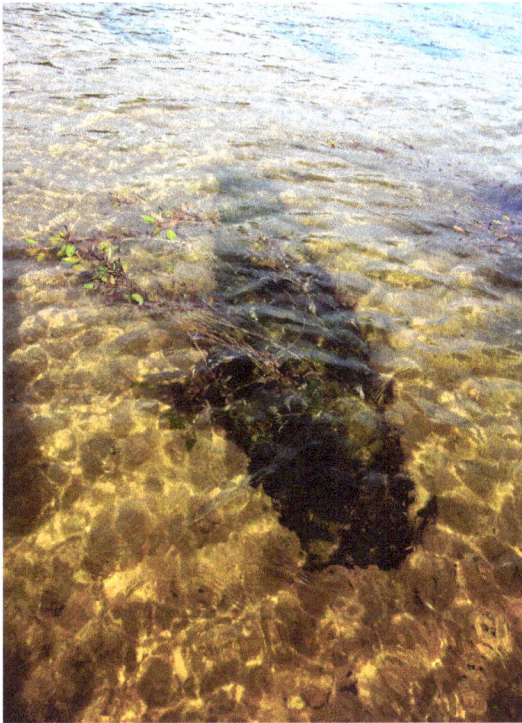

Grave hole on Kemper Flats, summer 2005

When a casket could not be located, a few shovels full of dirt were placed in the box, the headstone was placed on top if there was one, and it was moved to be reburied. Most of the graves from the area were moved to St. John's cemetery, just a few miles from the campground.

"When you talk about moved graves and unmoved graves, I can tell you the ones that are documented as moved, there's are a whole bunch of them that the people are still there. You can go out on Dale Hollow right now...and you can see rows of the old Dracula-shaped caskets in the soil. Those people were the ones that they took a few shovels of and left..."

Shell led the participants through an area that used one of the senses not often thought of when searching for ghosts.

"When you walk this direction, I want you to know I did talk about seeing, hearing, smelling –for some reason in my youth I walked through this area and smelled hay."

Shell said he would smell it at different times, even in the winter. It wasn't until later in life that he learned an old hay barn used to sit in that area before Dale Hollow was constructed.

"Keep your eyes and ears open," he told the crowd. "Please, if you get some orbs, show them to people."

No sooner than Shell spoke, many of the participants taking digital pictures began noticing unusual lights appearing in their pictures. "Wow, look what I caught!" one exclaimed in excitement as he shared the picture with the gravedigger.

"They're very common in this area," Shell replied, as he continued leading the group to another location.

Orbs on tour, 2007

"This is one of the places in the campground that I do not like to be," he said upon arriving at a turn on the road.

"Not because it's particularly scary, but it's particularly unhappy," he said, as a member of the group said, "It's right there, it's right there."

"I just got three right over there!" she said, as another member of the group proclaimed "oh my gosh!"

Several other members said they also captured images at the location, as Shell proceeded to spin the tale about the area.

"Let me tell you why I don't like this area," he said.

He went on to tell the story of the Watson family in the 1930s and young L.V. Watson, who was around twelve at the time. L.V.'s responsibility was to move the heifers from pasture to pasture as necessary, and he began the practice of tying the lead rope around his waste to make his chore easier and also protect his hands from chaffing from the rope. On one day, something spooked the heifer he was moving.

"As his family watched, his poor little legs couldn't keep up just right about here," Shell said. "And his family watched him be trampled to death."

Shell said the community stopped entirely as it mourned the death of the young lad.

"I never did like it here anyway," he said. "As we march on just a little ways further, we'll get to a lot happier place."

The group continued on their tour, as tree frogs and crickets ushered them on their way. Shell halted them to continue spinning his web.

He told of the Willow Grove Church of Christ that stood in the area before the creation of the lake, roughly where the swimming area stands today. He said 11 people were buried behind the church; most of them were women and children that died during the childbirth process.

"I will say now that most of the time when I get orb pictures down there, they usually do come in one large and one small."

Shell continued his web of tales, telling next of the Willow Grove schoolhouse, which was also in the area before the creation of the lake. He said the school had a very good basketball team, and many would travel by horseback to see the games.

He told of Edward and Sarah Irons, the namesake for Irons Creek just out from Willow Grove Resort. The couple had a twin son and daughter. Rachel, their daughter, grew up and married William Dale. Dale owned 449 acres, for which Dale Hollow was named. The other twin was an avid horse rider and in 1799, when he was 18, he would race the horse through the area.

"He just happened to take that horse a little too close to a walnut tree, and that child's head hit a low-lying tree limb and killed him instantly.

"...Edward Irons, despite as depressed as he was, he took his axe and he cut down that tree. And he cut, and he planed, and he sawed boards to make a casket for his son out of that tree."

Shell said he buried his son on a shaley knoll, overlooking the river that was present at the time, a place he had chosen for his own burial.

"That would be an interesting enough story on its own," he continued. "But about 100 years later the city of Willow Grove began and sort of evolved slowly. And they said, 'you know what, we need us a log building here for a school,' so they started scraping off some of the dirt and low and behold they find this walnut casket. It was such a shaley, dry soil that even 100 years later it was still there."

The townspeople started questioning who was in the grave, and it was determined it was Edward Irons' son, believed to be named Eddie. It was decided he would be reburied at the site.

"About 30 years later, they outgrew their school," Shell said. "They started excavating for a new school, a bigger school. Low and behold they scratch up a walnut casket still just as dry and as good as it was originally."

Shell said the town folk again wondered what to do with the casket. It was decided he would be reburied again at the site.

Irons Grave, 1930s

The need for more space came again in 1936, and once again a new school was to be built. And yet once again Eddie Irons was dug up during the creation of the school. This time it was decided to rebury him again at the site, only this time he was to be buried within the concrete steps of the school.

"That's a great idea," Shell said the people of community felt. "Now he's a monument. And that's what he was. The people of Willow Grove by now they knew this was Iron's Creek, that's the Irons' boy, this is a monument to the city of Willow Grove. He'll be there forever."

But in 1942, Shell said the Corps of Engineers began building the lake and dynamited the steps in hopes of removing Eddie Irons. But Eddie didn't want to leave.

Shell said he is documented as being grave 106 moved from Willow Grove to St. John's Cemetery, listed as an "unknown grave." But in reality the steps are more or less still in the depths of the Willow Grove area of the lake, and some divers have documented the steps with underwater camera equipment.

"So I can tell you now that Mr. Eddie Irons is still down there in the lake right where we swam. So think about him when you're swimming out there."

Shell led the group back through his web of stories to the gatehouse, where the adventure began.

It was a history lesson to some. It was ghost stories to others. One thing for sure, it was enlightening for all who participated.

Darren Shell can be found running his family business at Willow Grove Resort when he's not digging up graves. He is the author of several books, including, Stories From Dale Hollow, The Gravedigger's Guide To Dale Hollow Lake, Haunted Dale Hollow and others.

Ghostly tourists from Livingston, Tennessee, fall 2007

Gate House at Willow Grove Park, fall, 2007
Photo Courtesy of Darren Oliver
Prints Available at Darren@overtoncountynews.com

*The Gravedigger and his 1946 Tour Wagon
Built by Larry Shell, 2007, 2008*

Gravedigger and His Tools of the Trade, 2008

Dale Hollow's
World Record Smallmouth Bass

In July of 1955, Mr. D. L. Hayes of Leitchfield, KY, caught one massive smallmouth bass weighing in at an enormous 11 pounds and 15 ounces. It was instantly recognized as our World Record.

Of course, Hayes was ecstatic. He had been trolling his pearl-colored bomber that fateful day when he snagged the monstrous fish. News traveled fast, and photos circulated the lake like wild fire. It was hard to believe—world record caught right here on Dale Hollow. Soon, both states of TN and KY would lay claim to the special smallie, as the name D. L. Hayes became familiar to most every fisherman's abode across the nation. *NEW WORLD RECORD.*

*D. L. Hayes with his 11 pound and 15 ounce
Smallmouth Bass, July, 1955*

As the years passed, rumors began to spread through the country about this fish and a possible tampering with the fish before weigh-in. Some said lead weights had been added to the fish's belly prior to its official weighing. Local guides let small comments about it slip here and there until a full-fledged investigation was launched, headed by the Tennessee Wildlife Resource Agency. Even before the results of this investigation could be tallied, The National Freshwater Fishing Hall of Fame, the International Game Fish Association and the State of Kentucky all denounced the fish of its title.

Overnight, Mr. Hayes's fish had gone from World Record to null and void. Although he never received official word, D. L. took the blow with stride. He had heard all the stories and theories. As far as he was concerned, his fish was a World Record—and that was that. In an article written for ESPN in 2005, free lance writer Taylor Wilson quoted Hayes on some of the fraudulent charges. When asked about the comments made about the oddly shaped color patterns on the mounted fish, Hayes replied, "The fish came from Dale Hollow—its mounted color came from Chicago."

Enough said.

So for a period of time, another large fish held that honor of World Record—another wondrous Dale Hollow beauty caught in April of 1969 by Mr. John Gorman. That 10 pound and 14 ounce fish held the title for a short time.

After the TWRA's review of the fish and its history, the Fresh Water Fishing Hall of Fame immediately reinstated Haye's fish as the record. Fierce arguments by then assistant supervisor Ron Fox helped in the reinstatement. But at the time of this writing, the IGFA and KY Fish and Game still do not recognize Hayes' fish in their records. Only the National Freshwater Fishing Hall of Fame and the Tennessee Wildlife Resources Agency hold the 11 pound and 15 ounce golden statue as our national record.

D. L. Hayes and his mounted record Smallmouth Bass

Regardless of what person holds what record in the clubs and associations across the globe, Dale Hollow has produced some of the biggest and healthiest smallmouth bass in history. Our strain of fish is second to none. And this Tennessee author thanks Mr. Hayes for his contribution to the history of Dale Hollow. ~

BASS Editor in Town to Research World Record Smallmouth Catch

By THOMAS P. WEAVER

HORIZON Managing Editor

(From the Dale Hollow HORIZON 2/9/05)

CELINA, TN-Well known outdoor journalist and BASS Publications senior editor Ken Duke recently spent the weekend here as a guest of Stephen Headrick to compile information about the world record smallmouth that was caught July 9, 1955 by D.L. Hayes on Dale Hollow Lake.

"Based on the evidence I have seen, I think the 'Hayes fish' is the biggest smallmouth ever caught," Duke told the HORIZON last week. "I am here looking for any new pictures that the people of this area might have or any other information about the fish that has yet to be recorded."

He said that any new photos or information would be published in the October issue of Bassmaster magazine, along with his updated article about the record.
"We will pay for any new pictures that we publish this fall," Duke said. "I hope there is somebody out there that can shed some new light on this story."

The story is one that has been riddled with controversy in the past. Hayes' record was in jeopardy about 10 years ago when it was challenged by a witness who claimed to have helped shove outboard motor parts down the fish's gullet before it was weighed.

With the new development, the record was removed by all the governing bodies including the Tennessee Wildlife Resources Agency (TWRA), Freshwater Fishing Hall of Fame, and International Game Fish Association (IGFA) in the mid-90's.

After an investigation by the TWRA, aided by outdoor journalist Larry Self and Ron Fox of the TWRA, Hayes' record was reinstated as the state record and as the world record in the eyes of the Freshwater Fishing Hall of Fame.

To date, the IGFA refuses to recognize the catch as the record in their books.

"It took very little evidence for the IGFA to disqualify the record," Duke said.

"Once time was taken to investigate the allegations, it was reinstated by everybody but them. If we can find out some more information to support Hayes' catch, maybe it will help encourage them to again recognize it as the world record."

Duke said there was "a wide array of opinion" when it came to the controversy.

On his stop here, Duke interviewed many who had knowledge of the catch, including the Roberts family who own Cedar Hill Resort, the site of the official weigh-in of Hayes' smallmouth 50 years ago. He also spoke with Hayes himself after traveling north to his home in Leitchfield, KY, with Headrick. He later talked to Jack Huddleston at Horse Creek Resort, the home dock of the late fishing legend Billy Westmoreland, and Westmoreland's brother Bobby.

Duke then traveled to Nashville to talk with Fox about his findings during the TWRA reinstatement process. The writer explained all of this was necessary in order to "find

the facts" about the story. "I came here to get to the bottom
of this story," Duke said.

Duke background

Ken Duke is the Senior Editor of BASS Publications, which
includes Bassmaster Magazine, BASS Times Magazine,
Fishing Tackle Retailer, and Junior Bassmaster. Before
joining BASS, Duke was the editor of Game & Fish
Publications, which covered 48 states with outdoor
magazines. Here the publication is known as Tennessee
Sportsman Magazine.

Duke's ties here come from developing a friendship with
Headrick. He emceed Headrick's fall Dale Hollow
Sportsman's CITGO Harris Oil fishing tournament last year
and has written several articles about Dale Hollow and
smallmouth fishing in the past.

CUTLINES:

RECORD CATCH-D.L. Hayes caught this 11 pound, 15 ounce world record smallmouth while trolling a pearl-colored Bomber here on Dale Hollow Lake 50 years ago in the summer of 1955. The fish will be the subject of a Bassmaster article in October.

Ken Duke, BASS Senior Editor

D. L. Hayes and His Record Smallmouth Bass, 1955

Writer's Visit Here Helps Reinstate Hayes' World Record Smallmouth

Ken Duke teams with TWRA official to convince IGFA

By THOMAS P. WEAVER
HORIZON Managing Editor

(From the Dale Hollow HORIZON 1/4/06)

CELINA, TN-After making a visit here to compile information to support the credibility of D.L. Hayes' world record smallmouth bass, which had been disqualified in 1996, BASS Publications senior editor Ken Duke has accomplished his goal of getting the record reinstated by the International Game and Fish Association (IGFA).

"It took very little evidence for the IGFA to disqualify the record," Duke said in a HORIZON interview back in July of last year. "I came here (Celina) to get to the bottom of this story."

Apparently his visit was fruitful, because the IGFA reinstated the record on December 12 of last year after Duke and Ron Fox, assistant executive director of the Tennessee Wildlife Resources Agency, met with IGFA officials. A news release on the Bassmaster website said Duke and Fox met with Mike Leech, ambassador at large of the IGFA, and Jason Schratweiser, the IGFA's fishing and science director, to discuss the reinstatement of Hayes' 11-pound, 15-ounce catch from 1955.

The website said the evidence presented by Duke and Fox "was compelling" enough for Leech and Schratweiser to give the record back to Hayes.

"I feel great about this," Hayes told Bassmaster. "It's good to be vindicated after all these years. I'd pretty well given up on it," Hayes said in the story on the website, "but you guys (Bassmaster) put the pressure on them. I thought something might happen after the article came out."

The article, called "The Case for David Hayes," was written by Duke after his visit here and was published in the October issue of Bassmaster. The story on the website said it spelled out the facts and circumstances surrounding the Dale Hollow record and the many reasons for believing its authenticity. Much of the articles information came from Duke's visit here.

He interviewed many who had knowledge of the catch, including the Roberts family who own Cedar Hill Resort, the site of the official weigh-in of Hayes' smallmouth 50 years ago.

He also spoke with Hayes himself after traveling north to his home in Leitchfield, KY with Steven Headrick. He later talked to Jack Huddleston at Horse Creek Resort, the home dock of the late fishing legend Billy Westmoreland, and Westmoreland's brother Bobby. Duke then traveled to Nashville to talk with Fox about his findings during the TWRA reinstatement process.
Duke also heard from a relative of the witness who started the controversy. Local resident Tim Barlow offered facts to discredit the witness' challenge, which originally caused the disqualification of the record. Barlow's uncle, John H. Barlow, claimed to have helped shove outboard motor parts down the fish's gullet before it was weighed, but Barlow's father, Ira, told his son "the fish was legitimate" and said his brother had fabricated the entire tale.

Because of John's testimonial, the record was removed by all the governing bodies including the Tennessee Wildlife

Resources Agency (TWRA), Freshwater Fishing Hall of Fame, and International Game Fish Association (IGFA) in the mid-90's. After an investigation by the TWRA, aided by outdoor journalist Larry Self and Fox, Hayes' record was reinstated as the state record and as the world record in the eyes of the Freshwater Fishing Hall of Fame.

The IGFA wouldn't recognize the record until now. Thanks to the efforts of Duke, Fox, and all involved, Dale Hollow Lake is once again home to the 'true' world record smallmouth bass.

RECORD REINSTATED-D.L. Hayes caught this 11 pound, 15 ounce world record smallmouth while trolling a pearl-colored Bomber here on Dale Hollow Lake 50 years ago in the summer of 1955. The record fish was recently reinstated by the IGFA thanks to the efforts of Ken Duke, BASS Senior Editor.

For Lily and Sally

A historical look at the old town of Lillydale

For most of us lake lovers that flock to Dale Hollow, the name Lillydale is most recognized as one of the lake's beloved campgrounds. The flat land occupying this rich peninsula is ideally suited for the many tents and campers that reside here during summer. Being situated perfectly at the juncture of the old Obey and Wolf Rivers, Lillydale Campground has fantastic panoramic views and wonderful sunsets to dazzle its temporary residents. It's a place loved by many. But where did the name Lillydale come from? To find the answer to that question, let's take a step back in time and see what we can see at this special location.

In the late 1800s, the juncture of these two rivers was a place of much commerce. Of course, at that time, this lake had not yet been built and the rivers wound gently through the farmed valleys and homesteads. Although much of the surrounding valley was a rough and tumble place, many still made this place their home, here along the winding banks of the Obey and the Wolf. In fact, the place was known as *Mouth of Wolf*, because of it's juncture with the Obey, here where the mouth of the Wolf began.

About that same time, the logging trade had grown into a huge business. Logging men floated massive log rafts down these shores from way up each river back down to Celina, Tennessee, where it dumped into the Cumberland River. Mouth of Wolf was a welcome stop for nearly all of the river's logging men, and each looked forward to restocking their wares here at the busy little river port. It eventually became a port for riverboats, as well. Colonel Armstrong ran a pier at this spot for the riverboat captains that navigated this shallow stretch of river. They would bring the many necessities wanted by the residents of Mouth of Wolf in trade for furs, game, and numerous other items to be sold downstream. This place was equally loved then, too.

But where does *Lillydale* come into play? Well, as the story goes, there were two young ladies that attended school at the Church of Christ building. The large, two-story building housed many local functions such as church, meeting hall, and school. It was a well known building recognizable by most that traveled the rivers and wagon trails near this little town. Its white clapboard siding welcomed many students and families for years.

But back to our little ladies. These two lasses were apparently the pride and joy of Mouth of Wolf. They had an inseparable friendship, and one was rarely seen without the other. Where Miss Lily Gilliam roamed, so did Miss Sally Dale. They were friends...through and through. And Mouth of Wolf liked it that way. That's what this story is about.

Aside from melting the hearts of this community's townsfolk, these ladies made a strong impression on their school teacher. He often commented to his friends and family about his affection for these girls and their always-playful and spirited mannerisms. And of course, they all agreed...he was preaching to the choir!

After some time, the school teacher began jokingly referring to the lasses by one combined name. After all, they were always together! Their name might as well be as inseparable as the girls themselves. He started calling the two *Lily Dale*...a simple combination of their two names. By and by, everyone else began doing the same. And soon, the one name Lily Dale became synonymous with the two gals the town had grown to love.

Then, our kind professor had yet another idea. Why not rename our town? Who likes the sound of *Mouth of Wolf?* Wouldn't Lily Dale sound much better? After all, what does Lily Dale mean? A lily is a beautiful flower. A dale is a placid valley with water. What could better describe this wonderful valley town better than a valley of flowers? *Lily Dale.*

Our friendly teacher's words hit home. The people of Mouth of Wolf agreed to change their name. They would become Lily Dale. After a number of different spellings over the years, *Lillydale* hit the maps. And the rest is history.

Lillydale Bridge, about 1940. Upchurch Family.
Picture taken looking east from Lillydale Campground

As most of our lake lovers know, the lake came along in 1942. The families of Lillydale were forced to move like those of Willow Grove, Fox Springs and many other little communities here on these shores. These closely-knit families moved from the homes they loved and gave part of themselves so many more families could enjoy this special reservoir. They gave us their home…their Lillydale.

But there is one more sweet point of interest in this story I'd like to share with the lake lovers of Dale Hollow. The Miss Sally Dale in our story was a descendant of one Mr. William Dale…*the* William Dale for which this lake is named. So, not only is this special lake named in his honor, but also by some strange twist of fate, he also played a part in the naming of this wonderful spot in the middle of his lake.

But now, old Lillydale is gone with only a few traces left behind of what was once a thriving little town. And although a campground now occupies the farm fields of old Lillydale, I still hear the occasional toot of an old steamboat whistle. I picture logging men along the old river calling to families on shore. But most of all, I hear the harmonizing chuckles of two little girls who's friendship changed the name of an entire town...the friendship *and name* that has stood the test of time. And I bet old William is still smiling about it. ~

Lillydale Boat Dock, 1948
Also known as Eubanks Dock

Modern Lillydale Campground

Excavation for the Lillydale Bridge, late 1930s

Lilly Dale School — 1936   Esther Clark — teacher.

The Ghosts of Graveyard Island

Between Holly Creek Marina and Willow Grove is a tiny little island. Over the years, it has been known by a number of different names, but after the Corps of Engineers deemed it a designated camping spot, it became known as Graveyard Island and officially hit the maps. Despite its ominous name, campers and boaters flock to its southern point for its wonderful, panoramic view. Its long shallow point makes swimming a breeze there, and fishermen love the steep river channel alongside. It's an A-1 place to play.

But, why would such a beautiful place own such a frightening name? The answer is simple. It was once a graveyard. During the 1800s and early 1900s, this island was just a high ridge along the Obey River. The river had carved into this ridge, leaving a high bluff that overlooked the old town of Willow Grove and the communities of Johnson Bottom and Willis Bottom. The ancestors of the folks of these communities were buried where they had a beautiful view of their "Bottoms" (so to speak).

As with many cemeteries of its day, the ground around the graves was heavily planted with a dark green ground cover called Myrtle.

Myrtle in springtime.

53

Myrtle Ground Cover in Cemeteries

This plant helped choke out other pesky trees and saplings and briars. Even in winter, the deep green hues of Myrtle color the cemetery floor in a rich carpet of vines and leaves. And in spring, it throws thousands of tiny violet blooms. It's a gorgeous sight.

S M i T H   T R A X 1 B 1 5 4   D 1 5 .

No. 36: Smith Cemetery

    Of course, in 1942, the graves of this cemetery (known as the Smith Cemetery) were removed from the soil and reburied at other cemeteries above and beyond Corps property. Forty-four large holes donned the earth that year.

    As with most graveyards, this one has its share of creepy stories. I don't claim to have seen ghosts here, but some have witnessed strange occurrences in this special little spot. For instance, one man claimed to hear the voice of a young boy in the Cedar thicket on the island. Yet upon investigation, the man found no one else on the island but himself. After some investigation, I learned that one four year old Porter Smith died and was buried in this plot. Could this voice have been his?

    Another story involved strange lights in that same thicket. It is said that odd, pale lights glow in the trees there, but grow dim and disappear as one approaches. But the mind plays tricks on a person in the dark sometimes. Maybe these lights are figments.

    Now here is a documented creepy tale. In 2004, four young men reserved the campsite on this point, joking with one another about the eerie name. One of the lads was quite a prankster. Before leaving on their trip, he searched online for a fake cadaver. I don't know where one searches for such a thing, but the fellow found just what he wanted. He found and purchased a rubber dead body that looked devastatingly real. With the help of one of the other young men, he concocted a plan and a story about a drowning on the island the week before, where the body had not been found.

Upon their arrival, the two quietly placed the fake body conveniently along the shore for the other two lads to stumble onto. Oddly, a couple of days passed and still the other two men had not yet stumbled onto this frightening rubber cadaver. Finally, after many beers and rounds of tequila, the original two pranksters elected to take their boat out fishing for a while, completely forgetting about their carefully laid plan and prank.

Meanwhile, one of the other two lads decided to walk off some of the tequila, leaving his buddy napping silently by the fire. One can easily guess what happened next. The wandering friend screams bloody murder, waking his friend into a panic. Chaos ensues. Cell phones sketchily dial out, further creating more panic…*dead body found on Dale Hollow.*

By the time the original two lads returned from their drunken fishing trip, the island was swarming with officers and paramedics and official people of every kind. Needless to say, our Clay County officials failed to find the humor in the prank, and carted all four men to Clay County Jail, where they spent the remainder of their camping vacation charged with public drunkenness, deceiving an officer, and the list goes on. And our little island gained a new story to tell.

Another type of ghost from days gone by is in view here, also. While gazing downstream toward First Island, one can catch a narrow glimpse of old Highway 53 etched into the rock bluff, left of First Island. The old road wound along the river and traveled past First Island on its journey northward. It crested the steep bluff between First Island and Stillhouse Creek. Its heavily dynamited walls can be seen descending into the lake surface. When the water is low, one of the old culverts emerges from its watery home and again sees the light of day after sixty-five years of darkened confinement. This road's ghostly remains are always evident. If you get the chance, the old road is still easily walkable from the Jennings Hollow side, and there is a wonderful overlook at its highest point. It's a must-do for true lake lovers.

As always, I'll end my segment with what I see from these great sites I write about. As I sit quietly on this red clay point, I neither see nor feel ghosts. I see the same forty-four holes dug in 1942 and the rich green Myrtle still diligently fulfilling its purpose. No, I sense no ghosts here. But I do sense the history these ghosts have left behind. The old inhabitants of this age-old point share with us one spectacular view. And I suspect it is like nothing they ever imagined. They saw no lake surface. They saw no houseboats, no personal watercraft…no rumble of heavy horsepower. They saw nothing I see now. But I sense their views of long ago. I see people and horses scurrying along the old road in the distance. I see the Willow Grove Schoolhouse nestled on the edge of town. I see young Porter tossing rocks in the river. And I wonder if he sees me waving. ~

Riding the Logs of the Obey

If one takes the time to drive a boat or personal watercraft up or down this long and wonderful lake, it is difficult to imagine that these winding hollows were once only a vast section of valley land with rivers and large creeks flowing ever downstream. It is hard to imagine that in the late 1800s and very early 1900s, dozens of hard-working family men cut and sawed logs along this river, making a living selling lumber all along the banks of this once-rich timberland near this pristine valley of rivers and streams. Men from many walks of life traversed these shores, living a life few could understand…and even fewer could endure. Yet, they loved it.

From the miles far above East Port Marina, to the last few feet of Obey River as it met the Cumberland in Celina, this long and winding, cool and clear, ever swirling body of crystal clear water provided a navigational path for millions of board-feet of hardwood lumber for decades and decades.

Logging Venture on the Obey, Early 1900s

These unlikely men knew every inch of this river system. Every shoal had a name. Every bend of the river was named and sometimes cursed in the often-harsh and rough bending current. These men knew the homes near shore and the families that lived therein. They knew where cattle could board certain boats and where high water could threaten downstream travel. They were savvy souls, crafty folk, making their living in the ever-changing currents of the Obey River Valley. And their voices could be heard far and wide as each turbulent bend of the river was navigated. Their long, bound-up barge of tied logs had huge oars tied to each end (fore and aft), which helped to keep the bound and staved craft from being splintered upon shore. Captains shouted commands to both fore and aft rowers, thus protecting both craft and those aboard from impending danger of crash. One of the most relished calls was "DO EASE", which meant "ease from rowing", or "rest". It was a call longed for by those exhausted from the river rowing. It was a small break from the ever-constant lefts and rights of the ever-bending river. It was a well-deserved break for those in charge of this craft's safe navigation. "DO EASE" was a joyous call.

In addition to the trading of the logs, often times rafts were large enough to actually carry the weight of many other trade items. For instance, chickens often made this long journey down the Obey, both for egg-laying benefits as well as a meal source of their own. Hogs, rabbits, and other wild game were frequently traded at river-stops. Boarding houses popped up at these locations early on, and families did their best to not only help those in the logging trade, but also prosper from their ever-constant trade of business up and down the river. There was an ever-changing and constantly-renewed flow of people along the Obey that provided commerce for these tiny and remote civilizations along it. It was a life source for these folks. The river somehow supplemented everything in their lives that was not already accessible. It was the stronghold of the entire community. And those that chose to call it home, loved it.

These river stops, or ports, became business trade centers in their days. Each special spot had its own different set of attributes. From the very upper forks of each branch of the Obey, to the last port near Celina, life was enhanced by river trade.

So with these thoughts in mind, I've decided that in this article, I would take us on a river logging trip. My historical views will be in the form of travel. We'll start at the juncture of the east and west forks of the Obey...East Port Dock. For those of you wishing to make a day of this...I suggest the breakfast menu at East Port's Restaurant. And, oh yeah, fill up with gas too.

From there (full tank and full belly), we traverse past the Taylor Ford, a designated camping area just down stream. Its location on this shallow red clay point makes it an easy stop where the old road enters the ford across the river on its way southward. Tip your hat to the laborers helping load straw on another raft.

We navigate a few more miles and find Sunset Marina. Is it time for lunch yet? All this rowing makes me hungry.

Shortly thereafter, maybe a couple of miles, the great Eagle Creek enters our river stretch, enhancing water flow and clarity in the river. We then pass Gum Grove with its red buoys and few houses along shore these days. Of course, we can't see them along the old river we are traveling. And shortly, we pass the Lower Harrison School in the mouth of Jouett Creek. Just watch the kids waving at us ruffians on this old log raft. Ah, to be young again.

Soon, we pass Armstrong's Pier at the town of Lillydale. Colonel James Armstrong fixes the many "brokens" along the river. His port is always well stocked both from and for the logging folk.

From here, it's on to Willow Grove, our largest town on our journey. We hear the church bell sounding at the Church of Christ, and watch the kids rushing from pews to swings. I think I can smell fried chicken and white beans.

Now, we are off to Fox Springs, a small community at the mouth of Mitchell Creek. The little schoolhouse looks so quaint right along side the old wooden bridge. Just look at the fresh strawberries filling the tiny crates. Maybe we could make a quick stop and visit.

The next stop is the always fascinating Davis Landing, where Cedar Hill Marina is now located. Captain James K. P. Davis maintained his pier on this special point, and eventually married into the Dale family so prominent on this southern stretch of river.

From there, we navigate the Barksdale Bend, where the graves of William Dale and his wife Rachel Irons Dale once overlooked the river they loved. Now, if we could just jump this huge chunk of concrete dam, we could dump ourselves into the Cumberland.

And there you have it! Forty-plus miles of river enjoyment...navigated as if the names of old helped us along... names like Smith, Parris, Hull, Rich, and Kyle...and many, many others too numerous to count. Names like these filled this stretch of river like the trees they logged.

Normally in these articles, I leave you with my "Views" as I see them in my mind. But in this story, I will leave you with two poetic verses which say all that need be said. The first of which is a snippet from Tennyson's "Brook". Though quite old, it is brilliant in any age. The second is a poem of my own. I hope these poems touch your heart, and I hope that you've all enjoyed your trip.

"I chatter, chatter as I go
to join the brimming of the river...
for men may come and men may go,
but I go on for ever."

~Tennyson~

By the Light of the Logger's Moon

By the light of the moon
in early June,
I watched the darkness deepen.

When the light went away,
and shadows stayed,
and I watched the river glisten…

I drifted down river,
and felt a quiver,
as voices of old awakened.

I heard "Do Ease"
amid the trees
when I took the time to listen.

I heard splashing oars
and loathsome chores
as staves and logs were fastened.

"Tie those logs…
drive those cogs…
don't let those square knots loosen!

"We'll drift away
at break of day
after the rains have fallen.

"Currents will pull
our cargo full
of logs down the Obey swollen."

Now I wonder if others
would ever bother
to hear those haunting words…

To hear the men,
both now and then,
that waded the river fords.

To deliver logs
down river bogs
to feed their family fleet.

By selling wood
as best they could
by dollars and board-feet.

But I hear their words…
amid frogs and birds…
I hear that haunting tune.

As I drift along
in silent song
by the light of a logger's moon.

The Iron Stone

The Plight of Eddie Irons

Over two hundred years ago, the shores of the winding Obey River were a rough and tumble place. Most of the inhabitants of this area were still Native American Indians. But there were a few pioneering families that chose to call these hollows home. This story is about one of them.

The year was 1799. Edward and Sara Irons lived near what eventually became the old town of Willow Grove. The creek flowing through this old settlement still bears the Irons name…Irons Creek. Edward (or Ned) and his wife, Sara, settled the many acres all up and down Irons Creek that they had purchased from the Cherokee. They had two children (twins) that eventually became quite famous in these parts. Their daughter, Rachel, grew up and married yet another famous person…one Mr. William Dale, *the William Dale* for which this lake is named. He and Rachel settled the many acres where our dam is built. But this story isn't about those two famous folks. This is about her brother, Eddie.

Eddie was a fiery young lad, and he delighted in racing horses. There were few pastimes in this part of the country in the late 1700s to occupy a young man's life other than farming and racing horses with the neighbors and Indians. But Eddie excelled in racing. It wasn't until his 18th birthday that things went awry. Edward and Sara purchased Eddie a new horse as a birthday gift. It was a particularly spirited and fierce race horse that was only partially broken to ride. But this didn't stop young Eddie. His confidence and strong Iron will never wavered. He had set his mind to ride his present *on his birthday.*

As you might imagine, Eddie and his horse had conflicting personalities. Neither was willing to bend to the other's will. And when Eddie's seat hit the saddle, he and the horse bolted into top speed. Nothing slowed their pace. Thickets and briar patches tore at their skin and hide, yet both raced on. The horse would not stop, and Eddie would not jump from the ride. Both intended to ride to the end. On the outskirts of what would become Willow Grove, a stand of large walnut trees lined an old fence row. Eddie and his horse raced straight for it, not slowing their pace in the slightest. Despite the impending danger ahead, they still raced onward. Limbs began to brush horse and rider, making it impossible for either to see.

And then it happened. Amid the chaos of brushing limbs, Eddie's head hit a low-lying limb of a large walnut tree. The blow ejected him immediately from the horse. Eddie was killed instantly. Mother, father, and sister watched, as the family's heart-felt gift took young Eddie's life.

It was then that Edward Irons took on the hardest challenge of his life. There were three things he set out to do, and it would take every ounce of energy he could muster.

The first item on his list proved easiest. The hollow-echoing explosion of a 50 caliper musket rang in the air. The subtle thump of a falling horse was heard thereafter. On to number two.

Edward stood solemnly at the base of the lone walnut that so innocently took his son's life. In his hands was his largest and sharpest axe. He swung it with every ounce of strength he had, and it fell with utter satisfaction. Its razor sharp edge cut deeply into the trunk of the old walnut. After an hour of chopping, Edward heard the creaking break of the trunk as the old tree fell to the ground. For two days Edward cut. He sawed and planed beautiful walnut boards. He pegged those boards together into a casket for his son. And with what little energy he still had left, he completed his third and final task. He buried his son on a shallow hill of shale near his home. And soon, Edward and Sara moved away from the hollows they once loved. And time passed.

About one hundred years passed, actually. The now bustling city of Willow Grove had grown around the old Irons place. The town had decided it was time to build a school. There was a lovely little hill on the edge of town that seemed perfect for the building of the school. During the groundwork for the building, an old wooden casket was unearthed. It was the casket of Eddie Irons. The townspeople were perplexed. *Now what are we going to do?* What they did was simple. They placed him back in the ground from where he came and built right over top of him. After all, he might as well stay where he was first buried.

Irons Casket, 1930s

Another thirty years pass. It was time to build a much bigger school. And the people of old Willow Grove were watching closely as they built. Sure enough, that old walnut casket again saw the light of day. *Now what are we going to do?* It wasn't quite so simple this time. This new structure was much bigger. Large volumes of concrete were being poured, and bricks were being hauled in from miles around. This was to be the biggest school within miles. *Do we really want a body beneath our building?* The answer was a resounding yes. This fellow had been there longer than anyone alive. *Let's pour him a tomb while we build.* And that's what they did.

Willow Grove School House, late 1930s

Our friend Eddie would now have himself a tomb. He would be there forever. *Or would he?*

In 1942, it was time to build Dale Hollow, and all the structures on the newly purchased government land were being demolished…including the Willow Grove School. *What about the Irons Tomb?*

No. 106: Willow Grove Cemetery

The Irons Tomb was blasted with many claps of dynamite. And with much of old Willow Grove watching, pieces of the old Irons Tomb crumbled and fell. But the tomb stayed in tact. Many have asked why the Corps had documented a grave as moved, when it actually had not. And who is to say the Corps didn't come back another day and remove him?

This much is certain. The steps of the old Willow Grove High School are still just how the Corps left them in 1942. Scuba divers have proven that the south side of the steps looks sharp and natural. The northern side where the tomb lies is crumbled on the outer edges, but still very much in tact. Eddie is still there, folks. And I think that is exactly how it should be. Eddie's tomb stands as a reminder…a monument to the settlers of old that endured the many hardships of these rough and tumble lands. And I think Edward and Sara would be proud. ~

Willow Grove School House Foundation
Fall, 2007
Photo Courtesy of Dan Yeast, Louisville, KY

Irons Creek Bridge
Hawkins Children

The Gator Story

Introduction by Darren Shell

Early in the summer of 2001, the lake was full of hoopla about our little gator story. Quiet rumors began to float around about this figment of a few folk's imaginations. No way was there an alligator living in Huffacre Creek. It was impossible. I was the king of the skeptics, challenging each story teller to offer proof of the improbable resident. Even my mother and her good friend, Patti Wright, of Monticello, Indiana, were dead set in their belief in the creature. I reassured them that there was no gator there and instructed them to keep out of the moonshine.

But I should have known that mother knows best.

Soon after my conversation with the two, the Clinton County News printed the following story—and I had to eat crow. And that crow is a tough old bird to eat. I thank "The News" for allowing us to reprint their articles for all to see. They are quite a part of our history—and quite a part of Dale Hollow. ~

Clinton County News

July 5, 2001
Part one of three

Dale Hollow Gator—Fact not Fiction
By Alan B. Gibson, Editor

"Gus" the Gator at home in summer, 2001

Life is full of adventures—some good, some bad, some minor and some major, but adventures, nonetheless.

What started out this past weekend as a harmless "joke" with a couple of friends, ended up being a day-long adventure that had a little of everything needed to make it one of the most fun-filled, and memorable events of my 43 years.

A day-long excursion on Dale Hollow Lake with a couple of good friends was filled with excitement, planning, stalking, and adrenaline rushes—not to mention adventure.

We went on a gator hunt—caught the gator, lost the gator, caught it again, lost it again—and finally had to go home exhausted, but at the same time, satisfied that none of us had ever had a day quite like this one before—nor would we likely ever again.

The Gator Tale is circulated

For the past several months now, rumors have been circulating about an alligator-like creature having been spotted on Dale Hollow Lake, and while most of the tales put the "critter" in the vicinity of an area known as "Cope Hollow", near the Kentucky-Tennessee border and just across the lake from Dale Hollow State Park, it was a somewhat unbelievable tale to many.

Even with some "fuzzy" photos that surfaced a couple of months ago on the internet that could have possibly been a photo of a small alligator like creature on a log, that could have as possibly been taken on Dale Hollow Lake, without seeing the creature for myself, there was a strong doubt that what we actually had was a photo of a rotten log that resembled a small alligator.

In other words, the proof was fuzzy, at best.

As the spring and summer progressed, the "Gator Tale" continued to surface from time to time, with reported spottings and the usual logical explanation that the animal was most likely someone's pet that had simply grown too large for it's cage, and was released into Dale Hollow.

A warm climate animal, if there was a small alligator in Dale Hollow, it would surely die over the upcoming winter, and from time to time, an additional part of the story would surface that made it even more unbelievable—that being of reported spottings of the "gator" last summer and fall, meaning the warm climate invader had actually survived what was one of the harshest winters we've had in Clinton County for the past several years.

the "Dale Hollow Monster" or "Lady in the Window" folklore that I've heard all my life around the lake.

No gators here, despite the fuzzy internet photos.

Accomplices to the Adventure

This is where the story might begin to get somewhat hard to believe, so we'll just be up front at this point and say that while those of us involved in this Gator Adventure realize that we have been known for our fun-filled antics over the years, and when together, our reputation for being "serious" isn't the best.

My longest friendship has been that of nearly 40 years with Allen Smith, now a Vice-President with the bank of Clinton County, and one of my "cohorts in crime" from our grade-school years through high school and for the past 25 years of our post-high school adult life.

There isn't anything we haven't done together, especially if it sounded like fun and might make for a good story later.

One of our specialties is pulling jokes, and while the victim of these jokes are more often than not each other, we have been known to "gang-up" on an unsuspecting victim from time to time, which is how Saturday's adventure began.

The Joke begins—early Saturday

While spending the weekend on the lake, we were summoned early Saturday to make a short trip to Wisdom Dock to pick up another good friend, Fred Groce, who was yet another member of the CCHS Class of 1976 and has spent countless days and nights around us, on and off the lake, relaxing, working on projects and usually having fun on the weekends.

After picking Fred up in Smith's aluminum fishing boat, the plan for the day was briefly discussed and it seemed that Smith had put together an idea that sounded like a lot of fun.

Having obviously rolled this joke around in his head for some time now, and with the "Dale Hollow Gator Tale" still being circulated from one end of the lake to the other, Smith had made a brief visit into town during his lake vacation, to purchase some small, plastic alligators about a foot long.

With a screw gun in the boat, we decided how much fun it would be to attach one of these plastic gators to a log in the area where the gator was supposedly now living.

Then we'd go back to the cabin, laugh about our most recent escapade and figure out what to do with the rest of our Saturday.

The "joke" didn't last but a couple of seconds.

"Boys—there the x!se!wxx#ech is"

Traveling up the small fingerling of Dale Hollow Lake we refer to as Cope Hollow (Huffacre Creek on the map), we passed a couple of boaters and waved at a few houseboat groups along the shore as we traveled to the very end of the narrow area where our plan was to come together.

Smith said he had previously searched out and found the "log" that was in the internet picture and it was there that our plastic gators would find their new home.

As we trolled toward the bushes, downed trees and logs in the end of the cove, I remember thinking it did in fact look kind of swampy here and just a little spooky as well.

With the log just a few feet in front of us, Smith stood up and began reading his gear, reaching for a plastic gator, his screw gun and a couple of decking screws.

As Freddie and I looked ahead at the approaching target log, it was Smith who made the statement that would change our plans for the remainder of the day.

"Boys" then came a silent period that seemed like it lasted for several seconds before being followed by the words "there the x!se!wxx#ech is."

Fred and I both looked toward the log that Allen had us drifting toward, and the silence that filled the air for the next several seconds was almost deafening—sure enough—there the x!se!wxx#ech was!

We began a scramble inside that small boat, and for the life of me, I can't remember what any of us was reaching for or trying to do, but I'm sure the scene could have been a fantastic video on how "not" to act in a small fishing boat.

Smith dropped the plastic gators, as well as the screw gun, which luckily fell inside the boat, and quickly grabbed his digital camera, began clicking away as Freddie and myself continued to walk over each other and make our own excited exclamations about what lay in front of us—on the very log we were about to use for a well-planned joke.

There he was, about four feet in length, brightly colored, slithering off the log and into the water as he headed into a brushy area—probably to get away from these three idiots in the boat who were causing all kinds of commotion and probably were interrupting his early morning nap.

Sure enough—as it slowly swam in front of us, using its long tail and four legs—it was an alligator.

More jumping—more running around in the boat, and as Smith moved to the front of the vessel for a closer look, I grabbed the camera and began snapping more photos.

Continued July 26, 2001

Willard Johnson and Allen Smith with "Gus" the gator

A big net, a hunk of chicken, a towel and a roll of electrical tape, along with a short "tussal" in the water, and the Dale Hollow Gator is in the bag.

After more than three weeks of stalking and hunting that included at least a dozen trips to the "gator hole" on Dale Hollow Lake, "Gus" the gator is finally safe from harm, and resting comfortably in a tank full of fresh water with an endless supply of chicken.

Allen Smith and Willard Johnson were involved in Sunday evening's successful "gator adventure" and upon arriving at Wisdom Dock with the 40 inch creature alive and well in an aerated live-well on Smith's boat, it didn't take long for the word to spread about the "catch of the day".

With flashes popping and cameras whirring, the mooring area around the Wisdom Dock Lighthouse Restaurant was quickly a center of activity as word quickly spread of the successful capture earlier that afternoon.

The saga of the Dale Hollow Gator has been circulating for several months since earlier reports this spring of a sighting of an alligator like creature in an area of the lake known locally as Cope Hollow near the Kentucky/Tennessee border.

Although the existence of an alligator living in a fingerling of Dale Hollow Lake was somewhat unbelievable to most who heard it, the story took on a heightened circulation a few weeks ago.

In its July 4 issue, the Clinton County news published a report, along with several photographs taken during a day-long effort to catch the animal after three locals, Allen Smith, Alan Gibson and Fred Groce made several failed attempts to get the animal in their small fishing boat.

Since that story first appeared in the Clinton County News, several other newspapers in the Dale Hollow Lake area reprinted the account and two separate reports of the sighting and attempts to catch the gator were aired on Nashville television stations.

Sunday's successful venture came after several afternoon and nighttime trips had also produced results that were little more than the alligator getting another good meal, compliments of the group who have now become known in the area as the "Gator Hunters".

Named "Gus" by those who were hunting him, the gator's favorite food appeared to be Cagle's marinated chicken breast, and Sunday's nabbing of the gator by Smith and Johnson began with the careful placement of several pieces of chicken.

For Smith, the hunt began like the most of the others had, but for Johnson, a first time gator hunter, it ended up being a day he will likely never forget.

Placing a large net across the log, Johnson said that Smith had explained the plan for the day, noting that hopefully, while crawling up on the log where he had been seen more often than not, "Gus" would become entangled in the net while searching out the pieces of chicken that were being left.

After baiting the log with the chicken, Smith and Johnson, who were accompanied by their wives, Lisa Smith and Sherry Johnson, left the area for about a half an hour in order to allow the gator to approach the log without anyone being around.

"When we came back, I looked up toward the log, and there he sat," Smith said Sunday evening as he held Gus carefully in his hands and allowed onlookers to get a closer look.

Smith said that he could tell that the gator was being held on the log by the net, which had apparently gotten around one of his legs and prevented him from leaving the area as the boat approached.

"I think it was Allen who said 'we got to get in the water with him' and I didn't even think twice—I just jumped in," Johnson said, just before Smith jumped into the conversation and began reviewing their next actions that resulted in bringing the gator to the boat.

"I slipped around behind him and told Willard I was going to grab him by the tail, and when I had ahold of him, Willard was going to throw a towel over his head and hold him down," Smith said, pointing out that as he was now an experienced gator hunter, his plan called for him to grab the tail, while he instructed the newest member of the hunt party to deal with the "business end" of the animal.

"Worked like a charm," Smith said, "As soon as I grabbed him, he turned and hissed and just like that, Willard had him covered up and we had him." Johnson said that after the pair had subdued the creature, it briefly began hissing and twisting, but with a firm grip on both ends, it quickly settled down and seemed content to be carried to the boat.

Back in the boat, and with a firm grip on the gator's mouth, Lisa Smith was summoned to wrap the snout shut with several rounds of electrical tape and with that, the ordeal had come to an end.

In the mean time, the fourth member of the Sunday afternoon gator hunt, was happy to not become a first-hand member of the excitement. Willard said his wife, Sherry Johnson, spent the entire time at the back of the boat, as far back in the boat as she could get.

"When we started coming into the boat with it, Sherry was already back near the motor and she started trying to find a way to get even farther back," Johnson laughed as he repeated the story Sunday night at Wisdom Dock.

Sunday's successful gator capturing run had a bit of a twist of superstition, as well.

Wearing his gator hunting attire, Smith went after "Gus" in the exact same outfit he was wearing the first day the critter was spotted in late June—a black Harley Davidson tank top and a white cowboy hat.

It was also pointed out that both Smith and Johnson are employed at the Bank of Clinton County, while their wives, are both school teachers at Albany Elementary School.

Sundays successful gator hunt has also brought forth several more questions, including how "Gus" ended up in Dale Hollow Lake, and are there any more in the area.

A closer inspection of the animal by Smith, Gibson and several others who had reported seeing the animal earlier, raised the possibility that yet another similar specimen may remain on the loose in the same area.

"I'm not sure this is the first one we saw," Smith said, noting that the animal photographed several weeks ago appeared to be somewhat different in color and perhaps longer than the one caught Sunday.

It could be that more "gator hunts" will be planned in the future, if it appears that yet another gator is still living in the area.

Currently, several avenues of getting the captured animal to a proper environment are being researched by those involved in the capture, in an effort to not only get "Gus" entered into surroundings that are more suitable to the normally tropical environment where they are usually found, as well as insuring that it is better taken care of and away from potential harm.

Wherever he ends up, we'll be sure his caretakers are aware of his acquired appetite for marinated chicken.

Clinton County News, August 2, 2001 "Gus Goes to Camp"

Arrival of "Gus" at Camp Earl Wallace

Phil Glass, left, an employee of Camp Earl Wallace in neighboring Wayne County, examines "Gus" the Gator after the locally famous critter was delivered to the camp last week by Willard Johnson, right, and Alan B. Gibson.

The youth conservation camp asked to take possession of the small alligator to use in their wildlife show.

Johnson and Allen Smith captured the small gator recently in Dale Hollow Lake. Several attempts to capture the gator had been made and the escapades of those trying to net the creature, which was reported in the Clinton County News several weeks ago, have also been publicized in several area and state newspapers as well as on two Nashville, Tennessee television stations.

Camp Earl Wallace is a youth camp operated by the Kentucky Fish and Wildlife agency.

Raising Steam
A Real-Life Story of a Man & Woman and
Their Quest for a Sunken Treasure

Story & Illustrations by Darren Shell
(c) 2005

Over twenty years ago, Tommy Maxwell stood scratching his head and staring at a map. He was a plant foreman in Livingston, Tennessee, but his true passion in life was scuba diving. He had started the only dive shop on Dale Hollow at Willow Grove Marina, and his hard work ethic had served him well as he maintained both jobs. On this day, he had just had an enlightening conversation with an older fellow employee from the plant. As he stared at the lake map in his hands, he couldn't help but wonder if that old machine could still be resting quietly on the murky bottom floor of Dale Hollow. As he studied the ink pen "X" scratched into the Mitchell Creek hollow on the map, he could almost see the huge steel bowl-wheel of that steam engine powering massive log-sawing equipment. The loud whine of the steam whistle filled his inner ear. "Yeah," he thought to himself, "maybe tomorrow is the day."

Tommy's excitement this day had been fueled by an often-told tale of folklore. Legend had it, that during the building of Dale Hollow Reservoir, an old steam engine had been left behind and buried in the rising waters of the newly formed lake. Tommy had often fantasized about finding this old machine and making a dive site out of it. He wanted that old steam whistle so bad he could taste it. He had shared his thoughts about this old relic with numerous friends and family, but never really expected to find this age-old figment. Besides, finding a sunken object in a lake is no easy task...even an object of this great size. Scuba diving in deep, dark water is a challenge. So he put his mind to work on finding another way.

His thoughts and savvy intellect soon brought him to Mr. Larry Shell of Willow Grove Marina. Larry had an immediate suggestion for narrowing down Tommy's dive time. Larry offered to graph the cove in question with his bass boat depth finder. If some large object could be found near the marked location on the map, then Tommy's crew would have a much better chance of finding something in those murky depths. Nowadays, GPS machines and sonar devices would greatly enhance such an endeavor. But during those days, only the most simple of tools and technology were available for Tommy and company.

Despite everyone's disbelief, Larry quickly located an enormous object on the bottom of Mitchell Creek, right where the old timer had made his marks on the map. It wasn't long before Tommy and his wife, Linda, were preparing for their first dive in search of this elusive treasure. Tommy had expected a difficult dive and had planned an intricate system of ropes and lights to systematically cover the dark depths of fifty-plus feet of lake bottom. But, strangely, that system would not be necessary. Either by happenstance or fate, Tommy and Linda dropped their boat anchor, donned their dive gear, and slipped into the lake. They followed that anchor line to the bottom and found that the anchor had dropped directly onto a huge and shadowy hunk of steal. Could this large object really be the long-lost, sunken steam engine of Dale Hollow? The answer was YES! Tommy passed his hands over the round, moss-covered back wheel of the old steam engine. Even in those dark depths, Linda's voice could be heard shouting through her regulator, "WE FOUND IT! WE FOUND IT!"

The two anxiously examined the entire machine. Steering wheel, bowl wheel, smoke stack, and YES...even the steam whistle! Yep, it's all here.

Tommy and Linda spent the next few months diving around the old engine and investigating the surrounding area of the cove. It wasn't long before Tommy had yet another talk with Larry. It seems that these two men were not willing to let this old machine be a simple dive site. What if the old engine could be raised from the bottom and put on display for all to see? Why not just raise it?

Well, that would prove far more difficult than either man had expected. In fact, if either had known what all would transpire over the next year of their life with this machine, they might have just left it there for the fishies. But that wouldn't be Tommy Maxwell and Larry Shell. Nope. That baby was coming up...one way or another.

Corps Official, Harold Stone with Barge Equipment

86

After three failed attempts at raising the engine with every piece of equipment they owned, the pair enlisted the help of numerous friends. Mr. Harold Stone and his fellow Corps Rangers offered their help and the giant Corps barge. That would be essential in the recovery of this enormous one-hundred year old anchor.

Also, scuba diver and close personal friend of Tommy, Mr. David Foster, offered his assistance and his large air bags to help float the engine. David hauled his gear from Nashville and generously aided in the cause of what was now becoming an obsession with the crew of Willow Grove…raise that engine!

Tommy Maxwell Talks with Channel 4 News of Nashville

And so it finally happened. In the fall of 1987, after many hours of pulling and tugging, lifting and dragging, that ancient hunk of cast steal slid up onto the Corps barge. After over forty years of solitary confinement in the murky depths of Dale Hollow, the 1898 Frick Company steam engine felt its first rays of sunshine since its wood-sawing days.

Tommy Maxwell and David Foster Near Steam Engine

It then made a slow and deliberate trek up the lake to its new home at Willow Grove. For six weeks, it was patiently sand-blasted and painted. It spent a number of years on display in the restaurant at Willow Grove before making one last journey. It was a journey of about thirty miles, to Celina, Tennessee, where it proudly stands for all to see. It is housed at the Clay County Historical Society Museum, near the old high school. I welcome all lake lovers to visit it. I often run my hands over the back wheels, much like how old Tom must have years ago, when moss still covered this iron horse in the cool waters of Dale Hollow. It's missing the old steam whistle now, but most of the rest of it is just how it was sixty-five years ago when fire and steam boiled in its veins.

I am happy to say I was there those days and watched that old and nearly forgotten machine see its first light of day in decades. I stood along side two VERY determined men as they concurred one enormous challenge. And sometimes, when I view that old tractor in downtown Celina, I wonder, "Shouldn't that old whistle still be here with this old machine? Shouldn't it be here with the heart and soul of Dale Hollow?"

Well, regardless of where that old whistle resides, I'm pretty sure it's resting comfortably with the heart and soul of Dale Hollow…and I'm not just blowing off steam. ~

Steam Tractor in 1987

Steam Tractor in 1990

Cedar Hill Boat Ramp

Most of us lake-lovers have spent numerous days in the south end of our wonderful body of water. The clear waters of the Obey and the Wolf join together with countless creeks and streams to meet that huge concrete wall we call Dale Hollow Dam. For sixty-five years, concrete and steel have held back a reservoir of clean water and rich history. Our journey today takes us to Cedar Hill Marina to uncover what lies beneath the waves.

It's commonly known that the Roberts family has owned and operated the dock since the earliest of days on the Dale. Their family has held ownership longer than any other dock operation on our lake. Now under new ownership, the marina stands as it always has, but with new captains at the helm.

New owners, Jack and Nancy Corns, and their sons, Chuck and Brian, have stepped into the shoes of the many Roberts family sons and daughters from the past with hopes of continuing this marina's rich heritage. We all wish them well, and with continued support from the Roberts family, success is almost a certainty.

But let's look a little deeper, ya'll. Let's stand on the boat ramp and look out into currents of the Obey River, now deep in the dark depths of Dale Hollow. Let's step back in time and see what the old Obey has in store for us…

It's the mid-to-late 1800s. It's a cool morning on the river, the pale sunrise peeking over the mountaintops. Light mists are swirling above the lazy currents of the Obey. Nothing can be seen on the water, up or downstream. Only the quiet chirpings of the birds and frogs can be heard in the mist. A fiery young man is standing here beside us, his dusty trousers are damp with morning dew. The brim of his large leather hat shields his eyes from the sun. He's listening…

Ah…there it is…

From the shadowy depths of the misty hollows echoes the whine of a steam whistle. *Whooooooooo.* It's music to his ears. He closes his eyes as a wide smile tugs at his face.

Our fiery young lad is none other than James Davis, the son of a farmer and settler of the acres all along both sides of this river. His father, Matthew Davis, had taken the coveted Miss Elizabeth Dale to wed, thus ensuring his ties to the hundreds of valley farmland acres that bordered this river. Elizabeth's parents were the earliest of true settlers in these parts, owning the entire hollow where our dam is located today. It was known as the Dale Hollow…and still is.

Today, like so many days, James is waiting patiently for his job to come to him. He is an apprentice to the captain of this steamboat pulling upstream, having impressed the old captain with his hard work ethics and sound river knowledge. The past five years had gained him the captain's trust, and he stands here today willing and ready to live up to that captain's good judgment.

Whooooooo.

The old steamboat slowly chugs its way upstream around what is known as the Barksdale Bend, far to our right. Puffs of coal smoke billow from its darkened smokestacks, once painted a shiny black above bright white. And even though Father Time has tarnished the once pristine ornaments of this old vessel, it is still quite a sight to behold.

Whooooooo.

By now, other workers are joining us along shore, already tired from their travels. Some have carted large wooden boxes down the steep slope behind us to be loaded onto this mighty rivership. A number of goats are being led down hill as well, and crates of chickens are sliding forward upon a large makeshift drag pulled behind a mule. Cackles and crows join the raspy voices of labor men filing in from the ridges nearby. Morning has begun on the Obey.

Soon, the old steamvessel pushes itself onto shore, its bottom growling and grinding into the shaley shore in front of us. This shallow point has the best access of any nearby due to the quiet backwater to the right of us. The almost currentless backwater makes it much easier for our captain to hold the boat in place. But even with the ease of dockage, young James frowns at the shallow water that still must be waded to load and unload all the tos-and-froms being carted both on and off the ship. It's awkward and cumbersome, at best. James climbs on board, his soggy boots dripping with cold river water. The captain's Irish accent welcomes him aboard.

"Mornin' James, me boy…a right-nice day for a river trip, mightn't ya say?"

"Good morning to you, Sir," says James, tipping his hat and patting the captain on the shoulder. "There must be a better way to load and unload here, Sir. We all tire of cold, wet feet and soggy socks."

"Ah, you young lads always have grand ideas. If'n your head wasn't so full of that little Hestand lass from across the ridge, you'd be a buildin' your own pier here like your great uncles down stream at Butler's."

James scratches his head at the old man's words. His great uncles had created quite a trade pier down at Butler's Landing below nearby Celina. All the big steamboats dock at that famous pier along the Cumberland River, just downstream from the Obey's juncture. His uncles are well-known and well-respected men in their communities, and James has always admired their fame and good fortune. In his head, wheels start turning.

"I see your mind at work, me boy, but a pier is hard work. 'Tis a love affair with the river, boy…not that little Sadie Hestand. She's got you hooked good, boy. I see it in ya. A pier's no place for a lady, me boy."

"That sounds like a challenge, Captain!" chides James with a smile. "I've been lookin' for one of those."

The crusty old captain shakes his head and mumbles to himself, "… Greenhorn … Throw some coal on the fire, Boy! We got a river to run."

And that's how one of the great tales in Dale Hollow history began. Young James became Captain James K P Davis, of Davis Landing, right here where we stand on the Cedar Hill boat ramp. He and Sadie eventually obtained most of the Dale and Davis family farmland around us and filled these hollows with children, whose descendents still roam our ridges and valleys.

As we stare out over boats and docks now alongshore, I can almost picture large wooden beams stretched out into currents of the Obey. I think I can hear calls of crew men around us, and heavy footsteps on the old wooden planks. And ah … there it is … that lonely whine of steam piercing the misty coves of yesteryear.

I think Captain James and Sadie would be amazed at what has befallen their hills and hollows. I'll bet this marina would look quite intimidating to them, with its huge boats and lavish buildings. I bet it would look like quite a challenge.

But somehow, I bet the Corns family has been *looking for one of those.* ~

Cedar Hill Marina, 1968

Steamship "Rowena" of the Cumberland River
Celina, Tennessee

Steamship Celina

The Old Lady of the Lake

A Ghost Story. This isn't history; it's folklore.

When I was a young lad, I would sometimes ask, "What makes those swirling mists rise up out of the lake like magic?" Of course, I was speaking of the tiny whirlwinds that occur on cool mornings when the fog is raising from the lake surface. They dart and sway all about the fog-filled coves here in our hollows. I have witnessed those same swirling mists form in the late evening hours and dance over the lake surface with grace and beauty. It is a beautiful phenomenon to behold. This story is about one such mist that lived years ago...and perhaps lingers still today. I'd like to introduce you to our resident ghost. She is The Old Lady of the Lake.

Our story begins in the early 1800s. A young farmer and his newlywed wife lived along the Obey River on a stretch of rich pasture land. They farmed those few acres of fertile soil with the grit and determination of true early pioneers. They were quite poor but turned to their acres of soil to produce a bountiful life for themselves. Although he could not afford to buy his new wife a wedding ring, he vowed to do so later in life...when the time was right. And together, they worked hard, played hard, and lived a blessed life.

Now, this alone would make a pleasant story. And for the most part, our little farm family led a quaint and rewarding life. They eventually worked and saved to purchase more land, and even began a boarding house for slaves working their way toward freedom. Their tiny little farm became much bigger, and their life was richened in many ways. And for all practical purposes, this family lived out all if its days in the placid shelter of the Obey River Valley…just as they had planned.

But there is a tie to this lake that our farming family left behind that brings us to our real story. It brings us closer to the "making" of our lake. It offers us a reflection of the past and teases our minds with thoughts of ghostly apparitions…long ago spirits in our midst. This…is what happened.

Our young farmer gave a solemn vow to his wife on his wedding day. He offered one simple sentence to her, which he recited again each and every night before bedtime. Before dozing off to sleep, with the sound of crickets chirping in the night air, he would give her his promise. "Someday…someday…I will buy you a ring worthy of my love for you." And she would smile with appreciation and love in return.

As time passed, the farmer began saving money toward his promise. And as the young farmer grew older, he finally fulfilled that promise to his wife. He bought her a new diamond ring, far beyond that of what he had ever expected. Their hard work in life had paid off…and he delivered on his promise, just as he had said he would. From that point on, the bedtime conversation changed. He no longer needed to promise the ring worthy of his love. It was hers to keep. It was she that now spoke words of earnest. "When I die, will you bury me with my ring?" she would ask. "I want it with me for eternity."

The farmer's answer was always the same. "Of course, my love. It will be yours forever." And time passed. Eventually, the farmer and his wife each lived to a ripe old age. And just as he promised, upon her death, the farmer buried his wife with the token of his love…her wedding ring. Soon thereafter, he joined her, returning to Mother Earth. The life of a farming family in the Obey River Valley came to an end, and Father Time ticked away.

Here is where our story takes a turn for the unpleasant. The year was now 1942. The US Army Corps of Engineers had purchased thousands of acres of land, preparing to build our wonderful lake. The Corps then issued hundreds of eviction notices and delivered many checks for family farm land. Houses were destroyed, businesses were demolished, and communities were uprooted in the inevitable transformation from land to lake. And there was one more unpleasant turmoil to undertake…one more ugly facet that must proceed…one more gut-wrenching task that must be endured…the removing of the graveyards. And it was no easy task.

First and foremost, no one wanted the job. No one wanted to dig up Uncle John or Aunt Sally. This tightly-knit community knew everyone within its borders. So grave digging was mostly left to outsiders…rough individuals looking for more than their fair share for their hour's wage. Their gritty and difficult work landed them many *benefits* in the form of theft. After all, many folks who die are buried with prize possessions…boots, guns, belt buckles, even jewelry. And most of it never re-entered the earth during this grave digging process. It was a sad system, yet it continued for the lack of a better one. And despite vigilant efforts by the Corps…many less-than-worthy disenterrments were logged into documentation…and unknowingly left for the rising waters of Dale Hollow.

Now, let's get back to our ghost. Have you gotten a clue to her presence in our story? Have you seen the ties of old…binding us to the building of the lake? In case it hasn't hit you…in case you do not fear the souls of the dead coming back in search of stolen property…I will present it for you. I will tell it like it happened. Hold onto your seats, folks…this ain't purdy.

It was the fall of 1942, when Tommy and his buddy, Willie, took up the job of grave digging in the southern reaches of old Willow Grove. Both had been digging all day and their arms and legs ached with the pain of their day's work. Night had fallen and both had planned to work even later…in these dark hours when no Corps overseers would be gazing over their shoulders. Their pockets were full of shiny parcels as they dug.

"I've sifted until my bones ache," said Tommy. "I'm done for tonight. I'm beat." He looked down at the pile of small wooden boxes filed with remains of very old graves. "You can't fit a whole body in these tiny boxes anyway!" he grumbled. And he was right. The Corps had provided these small boxes to be filled with bodily remains of those graves too old to be dug in full. Many of these old graves could not be found, and even those that could, would not lend themselves to be easily dug. Their old and weathered stones had fallen, and briars had disguised their once lavishly decorated plots. Even if one wanted to dig these graves properly, it would have been most difficult. There was just very little left to dig…and sifting was the only real way to discern body from dirt.

"Yeah, I'm tired, too," commented Willie. "Let's gather our…" He stopped mid-sentence with a mumble of surprise. Something had caught his gaze in the dusty soil at his feet. Something *sparkled.* "Whoa…" he uttered.

Tommy stared in disbelief, as Willie pulled a shiny diamond ring from the clammy soil at his feet. Even with its great age and tarnished surface, it was easy to tell that is was of uncommon quality…and quite valuable. "Wow!" exclaimed Tommy as Willie examined his prize. "Put that one in your pocket, and let's head for home."

But Willie was too mesmerized by the piece of jewelry in his hands. *Gold…diamonds…flawless!* He quickly dropped it into his pants pocket. The precious metal of the ring was cold against his leg. Its weight seemed even heavier than normal. This parcel was different somehow. And soon Willie would know why.

Cool mists began to blow in the hollow. A damp and cold air settled in around them as they stood bewildered in their freshly dug graves. Clouds of fog gathered near and far…and they seemed to swirl in the night air. The once warm and humid night grew cold and damp, chilling both men to their core. "What's that?" chattered Tommy.

Both men heard something calling on the air. Was it their imagination, or perhaps just a whining in the wind? But there it was again. Strange voices seemed to call in the night air...moaning desperately in the breeze. And then both men heard words...real words in the spinning mists of fog. And those words were unquestionable. Four words seemed to hang in the air... "Where's my diamond ring?"

"Put it back!" shouted Tommy. "Push it back in the ground! Now!"

But Willie stood clinching the ring in his grip. He was too engulfed in the moment to consider his hand...or what it held. He was chilled to the bone...and for good reason. The swirling mists in the air began to take form. Those forms swirled into shapes of people...shapes of those folks from long ago. And they were letting their presence be known. Faster and faster the mists spun. Voices of old shouted and called. They swirled and swayed into giant whirlwinds of mist and fog. Again, one voice called out! "Where's my diamond ring?" In absolute panic, Willie threw the ring with all is might and fell to the ground with his hands over his ears. The ring landed deep into the grassy field near the old river, where it laid silently hidden to all. But the mists still called and whined all about. Whirlwinds would raise and fall in bitter dismay...ever hissing into the night air. Unrest and anger pounded through the night sky. The small whirlwinds began to join into one giant tornado of mist and fog. The joining cyclone of energy ascended high into the air and then crashed down through the cemetery with one tremendous display of crashing splendor...taking with it all forms of life, including that of the lowly gravediggers. And the graveyard fell utterly silent.

The whereabouts of the famous ring of our farming housewife is unknown. Many say that the souls of Dale Hollow still search in vain for this elusive piece of antique jewelry. Many say that The Old Lady of the Lake still swirls in the misty coves of Dale Hollow and seeks the token of love once given to her by her loving husband, so many years ago. "Where's my diamond ring?" echoes into our quiet hollows…even when no one is present to listen.

Have you ever heard that voice in the night air? Have you ever witnessed those special swirling mists that rise and fall into the misty hollows of this dale? Have you ever felt that you were *not alone* in our coves?

I know that I have seen those mists many days, quietly swirling their way over the lake surface. And I sometimes wonder…if they are really mists at all. ~

Just Sittin' on the Fox Springs Bridge

Most of our lake lovers of Dale Hollow have never even heard the name *Fox Springs*, but it was once a special little spot along the old Obey River. At the mouth of Mitchell Creek, where the lake now bends toward the dam, is the location of what was once a thriving little community. Tennessee Highway 53 followed alongside the Obey River from about Dale Hollow Marina, up through and beyond First Island. On its journey northward (against the current), the old highway crossed the clear waters of Mitchell Creek with one of the few bridges that the old road possessed. The old foundation pillars and wooden planks of the bridge saw a lot of history over the years, as families traversed miles of road and shoreline in the early years of the 1900s. These people loved it here at the mouth of Mitchell Creek, where days and nights were far simpler than the days of hustle and bustle of our modern times. They loved this rich valley land beyond the old bridge, where time now seems to stand still...only remembering those fond days of old.

In reality, we lake lovers can float comfortably in our boats and watercraft at the beautiful juncture of Mitchell Creek and the main lake, but let's take a moment to let our minds drift back into yesteryear. Let's view the times when life was simple. Let's sit ourselves down on this old bridge and take a look around. The old road is quiet today, and the currents of the Mitchell are lulling us into daydream. Ah, smell the honeysuckle on the air. Hear the scampering school kids racing into the old school house as the old school bell echoes through the hollows. Feel the cool breeze on our dangling bare feet above the cool and misty waters of Mitchell Creek. Welcome to Fox Springs.

Now, as we sit comfortably on this landmark of days long gone, let's cast our gaze up into the hollows of Mitchell Creek.

About a quarter mile up into the hollow on the right is the old church. Its white clapboard siding is slightly tinted with the shadows of the old cedar trees offering shade and shelter from above. Its tiny cemetery in the back is holding a few freshly-cut flowers placed lovingly by family members. Its bell also chimes through the quiet hills and hollows.

Let's look farther up into the hollow. With every bend of the creek, there are more and more little cemeteries. It seems that every other point has some sort of myrtle growing on the once heavily-trodden, but now forgotten sites of family burial. It's almost heartbreaking to see what was once a beloved spot now so quickly overlooked. But we see you, our fallen Dale Hollow friends. You are not forgotten.

Let's look even farther upstream. We can't quite see it from here, but I can picture it so easily. About a mile past Mitchell Creek Marina on the Mitchell Creek Fork, there is an old road that enters the water on the right. That cove where the road enters has seen its share of history. Aside from the heavily traveled wagon trail that now serves as a launch ramp, a wonderful cascading waterfall enters the Mitchell here. A couple of hundred yards up into the far left fork of this little creek is the cool and soothing waterfall known as the Mitchell Creek Cascade. From a dark hole in the bluff, a fresh flow of water eases out onto a long staircase of dark shale rock. These waters are music to my ears and these mossy stones are soothing to my feet. But as much as I hate to let our minds wander from here, let's look around some more.

Mitchell Creek Cascades
Photo Courtesy of Beth Shell

All up and down this long hollow, the name *Chilton* has plowed its fields and sown its crops for centuries. Every point has been traversed by the feet of a wandering Chilton. It is a little known fact that Chiltons were on the Mayflower. On this first voyage of this famous boat to the new world, that name graced the list of onboard travelers. Some of the very first foreign folks to these lands were Chiltons. They traded with the Native Americans and tamed much of the early American lands...especially in this hollow. I don't care who you are...that's WAY back.

But let's get back to our bridge. As we sit here enjoying our views upstream, the point on our left is full of people stirring. Most of the houses of Fox Springs centered around this point. The hand-dug well still resides on this point. Its hand-carved rocks are still diligently fulfilling their purpose, holding back the soil of this deep hole. Be careful here. It's a long way to the bottom of this one.

At the north end of our bridge is the schoolhouse. Chiltons and Davises, Rileys and Browns all scampered the wagon roads and foot paths to the old school that rested at the mouth of Mitchell Creek. At one time, the building was also the Clay County Board of Education. This well respected school educated many of the local families up and down the river. Shoot, I bet there's a Chilton with his nose in a circle on the chalk board right now.

Behind us now, the Obey is winding its way toward Celina, Tennessee. Mr. William Dale II and his wife, Martha Goodpasture, were buried right along side the river...here in the Goodpasture Bend, a half-mile behind us. It seems many of these hollows were *Dale* hollows.

Also behind us, are the long and bending paths of the Red Oak Trail. What was once a series of horse trails and logging roads, is now a long and very well kept hiking/horse trail. It covers many miles, winding in and out of the points and hollows just upstream from us. The entire eastern shore between here and First Island is a maze of fantastic trials with wonderful overlooks of the main lake. One can start on any point of this long flat and either wind along shore or take a walk up the ridge to view the lake from high above. There are several great places to view both up and down the main lake from the rocky outcroppings above the old river.

One of these rocky overlooks is still home to one forgotten and unknown person. That's right…unknown. It seems that this one individual still holds one fantastic eternal view of our little bridge and the mouth of Mitchell Creek. On one of my many trips up onto this placid trail, I meandered off the beaten path and walked out onto a splendid stone overlook. Few of us modern-day folk have ever looked out over the mouth of Mitchell Creek from this vantage point. Only those of long ago enjoyed this great view of the old river. But there is one fallen soul that still enjoys this special spot. One unknown person was laid to rest on this rocky overlook. A stone and rock covered grave still stands much like it did over one hundred years ago…still resting comfortably where this person chose to spend eternity. The dilapidated and weathered stones of this grave are barely discernable on that high ridge. But they are there. Those stones still stand as a reminder that there were others before us. There were people calling this place home long before we called it lake.

I share this person's special view every now and then. I walk up the old trail and look out over the vast terrain where there were homes and barns, churches and schools. I still see our pleasant little bridge much like how my unknown friend must have seen it many years ago.

So, when my boat glides through the waters of the mouth of Mitchell Creek, I glance back over my shoulder and think of someone I never knew that just might be looking down on me…and I smile. I smile because where this little bridge once was, is a very rich place to be, both then…and now. ~

'Smallmouth King' honored at Bassmaster Classic

Billy Westmoreland first posthumous Bass Fishing Hall of Fame inductee

By THOMAS P. WEAVER
HORIZON Managing Editor
(From the Dale Hollow HORIZON 8/11/04)

Many of us who have lived all of our lives here skirting the ban of Dale Hollow Lake have always heard larger than life fish stori but do we ever remember the angler behind the tale? Possibly n but there is one angler that we all know of and holds legenda status here around these pristine waters.

Billy Westmoreland was known as the 'Smallmouth King,' a lived up to the name while bringing Dale Hollow to the forefront the bronzeback world. Most never thought of l accomplishments as fish stories, probably because he was able show proof of his greatness on the water here and abroad.

This greatness was known in and around the Dale Hollow area i years, but it wasn't until the 70's when Billy broke onto the sce in the B.A.S.S professional circuit that the world took notice. I being a pioneer of the Bassmaster Tournament Trail with thi major wins in his six years of professional competition a qualifying for the Classic six consecutive years, he began professional career of greatness.

His tournament wins included the 1974 and 1975 Florida B.A.S.S. Invitationals on the St. Johns River and the 1977 Arkansas B.A.S.S. Invitational on Greers Ferry. He was one of the most consistent anglers of his time, earning money in more than half of the tournaments he entered and fishing in the top 50 two out of every three events in his career. Along the way he made a name for himself and the small community from which he came.

Billy Westmoreland and winning trophies

Dale Hollow became "The Smallmouth Capital of the World," not only because of D.L. Hayes' world record catch, but also because of the promotion of the lake that came via Billy's career. He was the host of a long running fishing show and penned a book called

"Them Ol' Brown Fish" that both tirelessly promoted his home waters and his favorite fish. These accomplishments, along with his conquests on the B.A.S.S. Tour elevated Billy to the celebrity status for which he is remembered today.

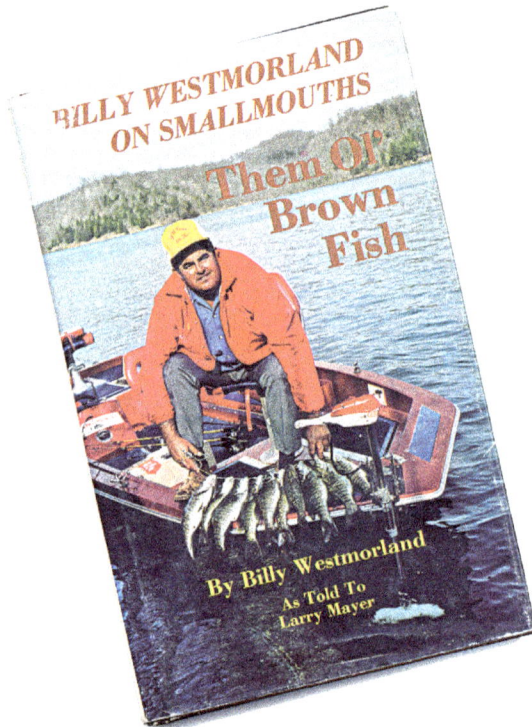

The local remembrance here has long been known with former induction into the Fresh Water Fishing Hall of Fame, but now his name will again be up in lights for all to see at the Bass Fishing Hall of Fame in Hot Springs, Arkansas. For the first time at this year's annual super bowl of the fishing world, better known as the Citgo Bassmaster Classic, that was held in Charlotte, NC the last weekend in July, Billy Westmoreland became the first Hall of Fame member to ever be inducted posthumously.

The Professional Bass Fishing Hall of Fame is a non-profit organization, dedicated to all anglers, manufacturers, and members of the media, who further the sport of bass fishing. They honor those whose contribution to the sport has elevated it to the professional level it is today. With these qualifications as a benchmark for induction, naturally Billy was chosen.

He entered the realm of fishing gods with only the fourth inductee class that included famed bass boat designer and former speedboat world record holder Earl Bentz of Nashville, TN, the founder and president of Triton Boats; two-time Classic winner George Cochran of Hot Springs, AR; and the man who single-handedly wrote the "rule book" for professional bass tournaments, former B.A.S.S. tournament director Harold Sharp of Chattanooga, TN.

"We are extremely proud that BASS invited us to be a major part of bass fishing's biggest week," said Bill Fletcher, president of the Board of Directors of the Pro Bass Fishing Hall of Fame. "The class of 2004 brings together both angling legends and individuals who help shape this great sport."

As one of these angling legends, Billy joined the likes of Ray Scott, Bill Dance, and Roland Martin at the top of the fishing mountain. Billy's brother, Bobby Westmoreland, and sister, Shirley Westmoreland, were on hand at the induction ceremony representing the Westmoreland family and to accept the honor bestowed upon their late brother.

Billy passed away back in the fall of 2002 leaving a legacy behind for future fishermen to follow. His influence on the fishing world will be seen for years to come, not only here locally, but around the world. He made a tremendous impact on the tactical approach to catching clear water smallmouth that has grown even more popular today.

With his famous 'Hoss Fly' jigs, he mastered the technique of catching trophy smallmouth and set the stage for the various types of hair jigs used today to target these thoroughbreds of sport fishing. Stephen Headrick of Punisher Jigs and his Pro Staff speak of Billy as their mentor, and anyone who has wet a line in the clear water of Dale Hollow will always wish they had the step up on "Them 'Ol Brown Fish" like Billy had.

Jack Huddleston, Owner of Horse Creek Resort, was, along with many others, one of Billy's closest friends. He and Billy were once business partners in many ventures, including Horse Creek. During his initial years on the professional tour, Billy carried the Horse Creek name as his sponsor and Jack recognizes him for helping jump start his resort business that has lasted now for over 30 years. Horse Creek has long been known as the fisherman's dock and that is just how Jack wants it to remain in honor of his long time friend.

Many others, including those he joined in the Hall of Fame, know what Billy Westmoreland has meant to the fishing world and Dale Hollow Lake. Now with this final accomplishment of being enshrined among the greatest of the great, those who didn't know the man will always know the legend.

Signature Splash of an "Ol' Brown Fish"

Unique Prospective

A tale of one of Old Lillydale's favorite residents.

Those of us that have spent a day or two in the Lillydale Campground know that the acres of ground that now hold tents and motor homes…were once a thriving part of the old town of Lillydale. A number of folks farmed and loved this long point that stretched out into the valley where the Wolf and Obey Rivers joined. The farmland that is now planted with campers and boaters once raised a bountiful crop of farm families. This story is about one such family that grew into harvest before our waves dampened their homeland.

This is the tale of the family of Mr. John Darty.

* * * * *

Mr. John Darty. Now there's an old name. Most agree that John's last name probably came from one of the old Daugherty (spelled many ways) family trees. But that remains a vague guess at best, given that none now live that could testify to that for certain. *Darty* was good enough for John…and good enough for the town of Lillydale. And that's where our story begins.

The focus of our story is John…and his prospective. John, without question, had a unique prospective on life. He was a people-person that loved his fellow man. He was well-thought-of in his home town, and the town seemed to relish in his family's presence. They came and went just like everyone else in town…which was strange for the day and time. Keep in mind that this was the pre-lake era. It was the 1930s. In other places of the world, John and his family would NOT have been welcome. Yet, the town of Lillydale considered this family one of their own. You see...Mr. John Darty was the only African-American man in the city of Lillydale...or Willow Grove, for that matter. There were other black folks farther upstream, but these two towns had none but the Dartys. Hence...a unique prospective.

Now...let's examine that prospective. As I've already stated...Mr. John was a people-person. He loved to be around other people and made a practice of being cordial all about town. Quite frankly, people loved John Darty...despite the darkened color of his skin. He was a beloved hometown boy, through and through.

John had taken a wife somewhat late in life. The two made themselves a home in the small hollow on the western-most section of the Lillydale campground (about where the bluff trail begins). They took up housekeeping and started a family. Their first child was a girl, with a young son coming soon thereafter. Mr. John, this people-person, was elated with his newly-found happiness of family.

It was then that tragedy struck. Shortly after the birth of their son, Omer, John's wife passed away...leaving this people-person alone to raise his young family.

But the town of Lillydale rallied around John and his family! John's children were as welcome in any home as they were in their own. Those children broke bread with the many other farming families of Lillydale, and the town thought nothing of it. Those two children attended the same school as every other child in the neighborhood. They sat patiently on the benches of the St. John School at the top of the Lillydale hill, just like every other farm child in town (the old building still rests along the old road to this day).

St. John Schoolhouse, 2006

So time passed. Our people-person, John, continued to live his unique prospective in a city that welcomed it. The city of Lillydale helped raise John's kids and all the local children came and went to and from all houses (John's included, of course). It was a great and wonderful system.

But to John's dismay, at a fairly early age, his daughter married and moved far away up north. As I understand, her move nearly severed her relationship with her family and friends of Lillydale...leaving her people-person father to live with the only other family member he had left...Omer. He and his son became almost inseparable...people-persons held together by family ties. They had an uncommonly close bond.

Then it happened. The lake, that is. The year was 1942. Our government had delivered a check...and an eviction notice...to John and the rest of the town of Lillydale. It was time for that inevitable move created by the building of Dale Hollow Lake. It was time for the farm families to pull up ties and move on...never again to plow the fields their grandfathers tilled. They would never again attend the same church service their families had enjoyed for decades beyond account. It was the last straw for the Lillydale citizens. And it was more than the last straw for John, our friendly people-person. He and Omer were moving on in many ways. And not for the better.

You see, Omer also had a unique prospective in life. Not only was he moving from his hometown by force. Not only was he the only young black man in a town of white folk. Not only was he saying good bye to his many good friends of Lillydale. Unfortunately, Omer also just happened to be eighteen years of age. And being eighteen years old in 1942 was not a good thing. America was marching off into World War II. And sadly, so too was Omer. So not only was Omer going to fight for his country...his government...but he also watched his government *burn his home to the ground*...leveling it to build our lake. And yet he still proudly marched off to war. Quite a unique prospective.

But before Omer left his home town to engage in that awful war, his father made one last request. He made one last strong statement to his son... "Tell me you will come home, Son. I need my family near. Tell me you will come home."

Omer had one heart-breaking response for his father...only one... "Just where will home be, Dad? Where will home be?"

For the record, Mr. John Darty never saw his son again. Private Omer Darty died in the conflict of WWII...leaving his father, the people-person, alone in the world.

Mr. John Darty eventually moved to the city of Livingston, TN, just twenty miles away from his Lillydale hometown. Each day, he would get out of bed and make his way down to the bus station and sit on the park bench...just waiting for people to come and go, so he could chat about their travels and perhaps tell a tale or two about his family in Old Lillydale. His eyes would sparkle with the memories from way back when, and many travelers would unknowingly share in the kinship of Old Lillydale...and the proud nature of this people-person...our friend...Mr. John Darty. ~

Purple Martin Phenomenon on Dale Hollow

As the last few snowy and blustery days unfold on Dale Hollow Lake, the shores and hollows will slowly be infiltrated by swarms of small blackish-blue birds. During those first few days of March, first dozens, then thousands of Purple Martins soar back home to the valleys of their birth (hatching, actually).

For some, this highly anticipated and much expected homecoming might go unnoticed completely. For others, spring hasn't sprung until those wonderful chirpings again fill the air. But despite the thoughts and views of many different people across this continent, these Purple Martins are here to stay. And to them, we should be grateful. Let me tell you why.

Our friends, the Martins, must endure many hardships each year during their many long travels. Most of this precious species makes its southerly trek to South America each and every year. Those harsh distances claim many of their tender lives on this yearly excursion, yet it is done annually just as it has been done for decades … perhaps centuries.

Martin Houses

Our many thousands of birds return home in spring and begin the ritual of rearing young. Each Martin pair returns to its nesting ground and sets up housekeeping. If Mother Nature and Father Time agree, those same pairs of birds will hatch at least one and sometimes two sets of hatchlings each year, with some of those hatchings rearing as many as four to six young from the same nest. Thus creating new life to fulfill the rituals and traditions of old.

That's where we landlords step in. As many of you know, my home is Willow Grove Marina. For decades, my family and friends and I have diligently maintained numbers of large Martin houses. People from all over the world come to see these simple structures that house one of Mother Natures true spectacles. They come to witness the multitudes of beautiful birds that grace our shores.

Pair of Purple Martins at Willow Grove Marina

These birds deserve more mention from me than just a mere stating of their being. These birds help us control those wide spread mosquito populations that plague our northern states. Granted, our climate is not as well suited for the mosquito crop like our northerly friends, but in all honesty, our other friends, the Martins, feed on these tender mosquito delicacies before the tiny bugs feed on us. Martins eat mosquitoes as a large part of their diet…thus making life much more pleasurable for us lake-lovers. And as a fellow lake-lover, I must say that I notice a marked increase in the mosquito population in those days in August when our little comrades fly south again. I miss them greatly the day they're gone.

Flock of Purple Martins at Willow Grove Marina

Martin husbandry (as it's called in the fancy books) is a difficult operation to maintain. Those that chose to build houses and maintain them are forced to uphold a certain amount of daily maintenance and time-honored practices to keep the home happy (husbandry…I get it). Swarms of Starlings are constantly trying to take over the Martin houses and destroy the nests and young babies feathering within. Those pests must be dealt with on a daily basis with ferocity and vigilance. Martins and Starlings cannot and will not live in the same area. You will have Starlings…and only Starlings. They don't eat mosquitoes and house flies. They don't teach their young to care for the home boxes in which they live (Martins actually do this!). Starlings are thugs that spread disease (ask your doctor) and louse…and destroy the boxes in which they live. They breed like maggots and must be eradicated before they make a strong hold. Those that disagree can look online and see for themselves. A few hundred Starlings were introduced as a small colony in the New England states back about one hundred years ago. Since that time, they have taken over many wonderful habitats and hindered many native bird species nationwide … all from a few hundred birds. But enough negativity. Let's talk about Martins.

Castle Martin House, Willow Grove Resort

Probably the most special of all the Martin traits are their sense of family. I know that sounds silly, but it's a fact. Over the years, I have hand-raised many baby Martins that have fallen from the box prematurely. After weeks of nurture and hand feeding, I would release them back into the colony. From the second I let go of the tiny birds and they flew into the air, a swarm of other "fatherly" birds would soar in around them and direct the little bird where it needed to go. They remembered the baby bird. Really! I've done it time and time again. The result is always the same. No matter how long the little one has been away...two, three, maybe four weeks...the others take the young one under their wing and take it home. It's beautiful. It will bring tears to your eyes...seeing this community of birds rally around a little baby that should have been forgotten...but wasn't. It's special. I count those moments among my many blessings.

Here's the one everybody loves. Migration. Dale Hollow is on the migratory flight path of the thousands upon thousands of Martins that fly south in July and August. Those enormous swarms of birds that can number into more than 30,000, are so large that they can be detected on weather radar. Our local weathermen know this and account for it in their daily forecasts during those months. No kidding. This happens! They will point at the screen and make note of the large green blotches on the radar screen, remarking that it might be raining there ... but it isn't raining water...

'Nuff said, again.

But the news isn't all happy. The birds do make a mess. The trees outside my cabins house many thousands of birds per day in late July and early August. The front decks of these rental units have literally been iced like a cake. I hose them off everyday in season to remove the trouble...but its back in minutes. Some guests are furious. They rant and rave and want to shoot the birds. But one conversation usually shuts them up. "Why do you come to Dale Hollow, folks?" I ask.

They usually reply, "It's one of the best lakes in the world...and there's no mosquitoes."

I smile and reply, "These birds are a large part of both of your answers. Think on that as I hose off your deck. Three or four weeks a year we wash decks. The other forty-eight...are nearly perfect."

So if you want to see one of life's true spectacles ... if you want to witness one of Mother Nature's purest of gifts to us as humanity ... come see the Martins. Look at the sheer multitudes of feathered friends soaring like clouds in the distance. Hear that wonderful chirp that fills the air with soothing tones of overlapping harmony. Bring your love of nature. Bring your love of life. And if you come in July...bring your umbrella. Come sit by me...I just hosed off the deck. ~

Swimming with Ortman

Despite this story's strange title and topic, somehow it has touched my entire family. I hope it doesn't seem disrespectful or morbid to some of you that have not been to this location I've chosen to write about for this article. That was never my intention. I only want to share history with other lake-lovers and show the beauty of the many places that this lake has to offer. Bear with me on this one. For some of the greatest experiences in life lie just beyond the norm.

My family has a special place on Dale Hollow where we love to play. We make a conscious effort to stop by a favorite point and swim when we are in the area. When we tube and ski, swim and play, we like to stop by and visit a friend or two on Kemper Flats area of Clark Bottom.

Not the least of our friends is Ortman. We've never met anyone else in the world by that name, but we love to stop by and swim with him. This little four-year-old has touched our hearts. His two younger sisters are here, too. Little Willia and Margaret share this shore also. Of course, most of the rest of the McCluskys are here too, and we share their spot just like we were one of the family. These folks always share.

But here's the twist. Young Ortman and his sisters died over one hundred years ago. Yeah, the McClusky family buried three infants and children in this old cemetery long before this lake came along or any of us boaters ever came into being. These lads and lasses loved this river even before we lake lovers enjoyed this vast and wonderful lake. So now you know our secret. We swim with the dead. Yeah, that sounds creepy, but it really isn't what you might make of it. For instance…

There is always topic for debate about the "moving" of the Dale Hollow graveyards. Of course, many were truly moved. But many were just too old to have anything left to dig. In these cases, only a few shovels of soil were removed. So quite frankly, no matter how badly a gravedigger wanted to remove a grave...often only a few odd shovels of "special" soil were taken along with the headstone. And that is exactly what we have here at the McClusky Cemetery...graves documented as moved. So no matter how black-and-white the Corps documentation seems to be, our friends at the McClusky Cemetery are both moved...and *not moved.* They are both. And that is where my heart lies. And Ortman lies there, too, for the record.

Grave of James McClusky, McClusky Cem.

Which brings me to a strange and touching thought I'd like to share. Ortman's two sisters share a special memorial plaque that adorns my wall. The family descendants have donated it to my tiny history wall in my office here at Willow Grove. I now care for the special plaque created by the McClusky family for the loss of their first two children. I happily display it for all to see. But young Ortman lived long enough to have his own headstone. And that perplexes me. Because I often visit him high on the hill at his headstone at St. John Cemetery above Lillydale Campground. But mostly, I enjoy his *spirit* out on the Kemper Flats at the old McClusky Cemetery. He and his sisters are easily found. Just look for the little spirits in the clay. They are side-by-side for eternity...or at least until our lake waves wash them into oblivion. So I suggest you do what my family does. Go visit young Ortman and his family. Do it before they wash away. They are patiently waiting for your visit...and perhaps a swim. They don't talk much, but they have plenty to share. ~

Multiple Graves At McClusky Cemetery, 2005

Graves, McClusky Cemetery

Author at McClusky Cemetery, 2005

Here is a little poem I wrote a few years ago when I took my first swim with the McCluskys...long before I knew who they were. I now know the answers to my questions.

Clark Bottom Cemetery

As I step from boat to shore,
And on to age-old graves,
I wonder...were you farmers,
Housewives, children, slaves?

And I wonder, could you have known
About this dam they'd build?
The dam that covered this land in water,
The land your fathers tilled.

I wonder if...knowing now...
What you didn't know then,
Would you change your resting place,
This shoreline you're within?

Would you choose to remove yourselves
From this shallow shore?
Would you move your age-old rottings
From this place you once adored?

Would you remove your contribution
From this clay you knew so well?
Would you allow some foreign plants
To intrude your fertile soil?

So, would you move, if you could?
If you were given a chance?
I, for one, would not displant you
From this ground that you've enhanced.

Hundreds have swam and walked above
Your unknown watery graves.
And, most have no idea
Of the contribution that you gave.

But, in my heart, resides a love
That I cannot explain...
A tender-hearted understanding
Of your hardships and your pain.

I think of you, my unknown friends,
When o'er your water I go.
I think your shore's a wonderful place,
And I just thought you should know...

That when my number's called,
And I ascend above,
That I just might be joining you...
In this place that you once loved.

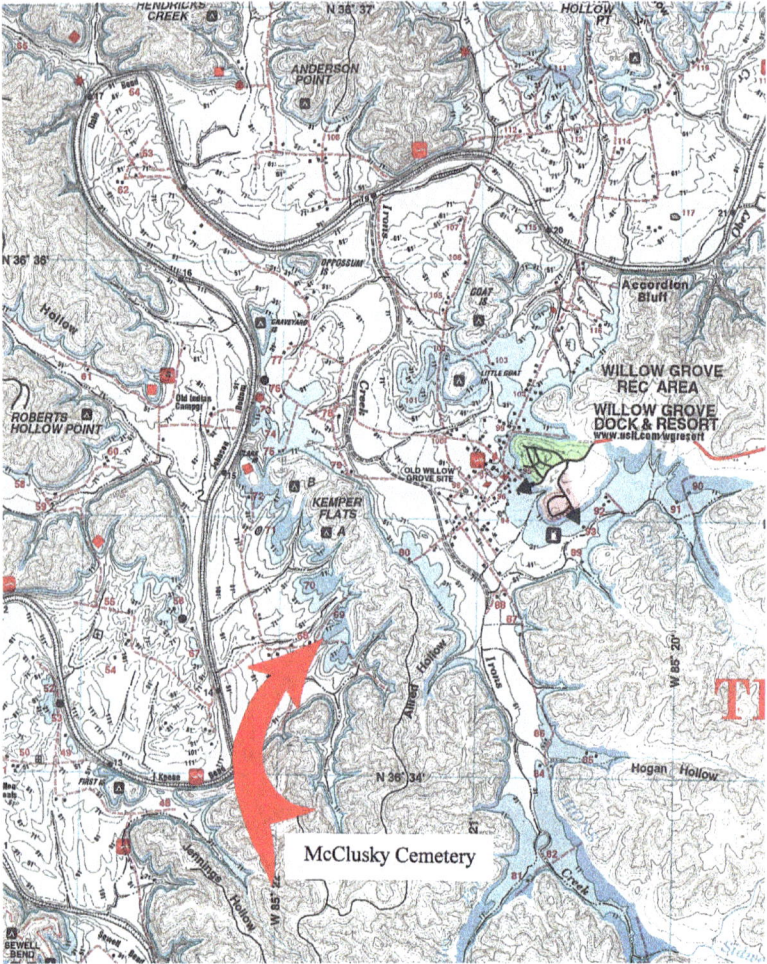

McClusky Cemetery

Old Sulphur Cemetery

Some may wonder why I often write about the cemeteries on Dale Hollow. After all, it is a morbid subject. But when asked, my answer is always the same. "There is a lot of history in the ground there."

It's not death and suffering that draws me to these spots. It's all the wonderful history buried there that intrigues me. Countless stories are buried there, too.

When I first found the McClusky Cemetery on Kemper Flats, I was overwhelmed with others that wanted to see that special spot. People I didn't know came to me asking for directions, and returning with a true appreciation of what lies beneath the red clay of that point. Thousands walked that shoreline viewing the odd casket shapes in the soil.

But unfortunately, the drought of last summer and the first few harsh rains of the winter have virtually washed away the shapes we once saw in the clay. Now, only crude sunken holes remain where those fresh clay castings once lined that point in rows. If you've never seen it, I suggest you go soon. It won't be there much longer. Time and Mother Nature will have washed it away, just as they washed it into view.

This little article is for those of you that have been to that old cemetery and have an appreciation for it. There's another on Dale Hollow you can go see. There are shapes in the clay there, too. They are a little harder to see, but they are certainly there. I'm talking about Old Sulphur Cemetery. It's a neat one.

No. 88: Old Sulphur Cemetery

Finding this spot is easy.   Just south of Sulphur Creek Marina is Casey Creek Hollow.   Casey Creek is on the western shore of Sulphur Creek and is clearly marked by one of the old white Corps signs.   Just below that sign is where some of the old cemetery shapes can be seen in the clay.   The graves are probably about ten feet deep at full pool.   So, if the water is down at all, even a few feet, the graves can be seen beneath the lake surface.   In the fall, those shapes are well out of the water.

That point is covered in dark black shale rock.   Nestled within this dark cluster of shale are pockets of red clay.   These pockets are the holes of graves.   Some are square in shape, while others still hold their "Dracula-shaped" coffin configurations. Some of the black shale still holds its shape, too.   Those were placed on top of the caskets during burial.   The shale helped keep critters from digging into the shallow graves.   There is very little soil depth in our hollows of Tennessee and Kentucky, and often graves are covered in rock for that purpose.   In some cases, folks couldn't dig deep enough without hitting rock to fully bury a casket. They'd pile on slabs of rock to cover what couldn't be covered in soil.

When the lake was built, 116 graves were moved from this spot and reentered at Webb Cemetery just north of the lake. There were Johnsons and Coops, Spears and Hoots, all buried here in this little hollow on Sulphur Creek's western shore. Although only a few holes are evident on the Casey Creek point, many more lay beneath the lake surface of Casey Creek.

As I mentioned earlier, history is buried here. For instance, old George Coops ran a general store in the Sulphur Creek hollow. Beneath Sulphur Creek's row of houseboat slips is where the store was located. Below dozens of lavish houseboats, a cluster of homes and buildings stood as part of the city once known as Peytonsburg.

The homes and barns of Peytonsburg filled the Sulphur Creek hollow west of the marina. Foundation stones can still be seen in piles throughout that hollow when the water is down in late summer. Miles of pasture land filled this whole cove from Diver's Island, to beyond the marina. Farmhouses dotted the long and winding ribbon of Sulphur Creek waters as far as the eye could see. The old road still winds down into the Casey Creek hollow as it did decades ago, when a different group of people called these hollows home…before Peytonsburg became just another wonderful cove in Dale Hollow.

So check it out. Go see that remarkable little point. Yeah, it's a graveyard, but it's more than that. As I mentioned before, there's a lot of history there. You'll feel it, I promise. That's why they call me The Gravedigger. ~

Old Sulphur Cemetery Grave, Fall, 2007

Old Sulphur Cemetery Grave, Fall, 2007

Early Houseboating on Dale Hollow

One quick glance at the many vast and diverse varieties of houseboats here on the lake, and it is hard to imagine how primitive some of the early houseboats on the lake were. From the earliest of years on Dale Hollow, houseboats have played a big part of recreational boating for fishermen and boating enthusiasts. With a look at the many beautiful and gigantic houseboats that now grace our shores, one might never believe what once floated in our coves. These old houseboats had no tracking satellites. They had no lavish hot tubs. Their biggest amenity was that they did float and offered some simple amount of protection from the elements.

Some of the early boats consisted of a wooden platform floating on used 55 gallon drums. Then, a small camper would set nicely in the center (high tech).

Edwards Houseboat at Holly Creek

Some other interesting boats were fashioned by facilities like the Westmoreland and Stevens Companies out of Celina. Those early Westmoreland and Stevens boats made up most of the early rental fleets in the marinas. This one is one of the earliest.

Lester Westmoreland's Houseboat

Still other boats were hand-fashioned and were as unique as the folks who built them. Some took on some strange shapes and had many odd forms of propulsion. No two were the same in those days!

Paul McComa's houseboat was cutting-edge technology!

It's difficult to tell where the many different trends will lead in the future of houseboating, but if the styles of the past reflect the diverse future of the industry, then we may have many interesting styles and shapes to look forward to! Who knows...maybe that old paddle-wheel may come back into style. ~

Modern Day Houseboating

Gold in Them Thar Hills

Some of us are born treasure hunters. We might not all be miner-forty-niners, but most of us enjoy a good treasure hunt. From Flea market finds, to fishing and hunting, an elusive treasure intrigues us all. That being said, I'd like to share a neat old treasure story with you. Let's talk about stolen gold!

I just knew that would get ya! I'd like to tell you the story of The Spanish Gold of old Willow Grove. This stash of buried treasure has eluded the best of hunters for decades. Our tale begins in the mid-1800s.

Just as the inundated city of Willow Grove was coming of age, the winding Obey River stretched for miles through our pleasant valleys. It was a chief mode of transportation for people from all walks of life.

On this day, three unlikely souls furiously paddled a stolen canoe downstream. These companions were an early form of guerrillas. They were thugs from south Texas or northern Mexico. They were part of the reason the US was entering the War with Mexico. Aside from the troubles the country was facing with Texas and its attempts to succeed from the Union, there were small bands of ruffians ransacking the remote villages along many waterways like the Obey River. They would steal what they could from these small communities and quickly paddle their way downstream toward their southern homes…thieving all the way.

But unfortunately for our three land pirates, they had pilfered and pillaged just a little too much. Their heavily laden canoe was full of ill-gotten gains, and a posse of local boys had started their own band of treasure hunters. And they had only one treasure in mind…a canoe full of stolen goods and three Spaniards.

This is where it gets ugly. As the story goes, the three were certain the posse was hot on their trail. They elected to hide their gold along the river to make a faster escape. They supposedly edged their canoe onto the rocky bank of a large landmark. It was a huge bluff, recognizable from a long distance. It was a place that these three foreigners could easily remember on a later return.

This ford in the river at the base of this bluff was a troublesome spot. Those traveling the old road would have to ford the river here to get around the steep bluff. In cold weather, or in times of heavy rains, that ford was not capable of being crossed. In these times, a steep trail leading over the mountain was the only path available. The sharp incline of that trail was no easy path to travel, but it was the only route past the bluff. That is where these lads took their leave.

It is said that these men buried their golden treasure on this hillside. It is also said that this is where the posse caught up with them. The waters of the Obey ran red with the blood of Spanish thugs. And time passed.

For decades, rumors of Spanish gold circulated through old Willow Grove and Lillydale. For years, people dug for treasure on what became known as The Spanish Trail. For decades, shovels and sifters littered the hillside overlooking the Obey. It wasn't until the fall of old Willow Grove that the first clue of the treasure was unearthed.

During the demolition of Willow Grove, during the making of Dale Hollow, dozers rumbled far and wide as trees and houses were leveled. On weekends, those dozers sat idle across the landscape. During the summer of 1942, a pair of local boys *commandeered* one of those idle bulldozers. They pushed away at the soil high on that trail. What they discovered was interesting.

Those boys unearthed a hatchet blade. The sides of this ancient metal icon were engraved with Spanish writing...thus proving to the local folklorists that there were indeed Spaniards wandering the early hillsides of old Willow Grove. Those same Spaniards probably left their gold, too.

Unfortunately, that old hatchet has gone amiss. No one knows where that fascinating hunk of cast steel resides. No one knows what those inscriptions once spelled. And once again...time has passed along the shores of the Obey River Valley.

Now, for you history buffs and searchers of local "treasure", this trail holds another fascinating tale to tell. Near the top of this trail on the eastern slope, lives a wonderful old tree. A beech tree of giant proportions stands tall as a reminder to local folks. This tree has many inscriptions carved into its silvery bark. Not the least of which is a name. One Mr. G. W. Sevier, Jr., has carved his name into this bark. And here's the kicker. He carved it in 1899. It is suggested that this tree is the marked location of the death of Mr. Sevier's father...G. W. Sevier, Sr. He was a Civil War soldier returning home from duty. Only a few short miles from his home, he was bushwhacked by enemy fire. As he was coming home from battle, he was killed on the friendly slopes of his own hometown hills. It is said that George Washington Sevier, Jr. carved his own initials here to mark the location of his father's death. It was a healing process for him.

Of course, this is only speculation. No one alive knows for certain. The Sevier family tends to believe the story as I've told it. I know this...I feel something when I touch that silver bark of that centuries old wooden statue high on that hill. It might be George. It might be the lost souls of three Spaniards telling me where to look for that elusive stash of stolen treasure. And it might be my overactive imagination stirring my emotions. But I know this…I like it there. That old trail is just full of history.

So, if you want to hike that old path, I've included a map. That old trail is all grown up with forest. The terrain is remarkably steep. It's no joy ride. But it's a neat place.

I suggest taking entry on the Pulsey Creek side. The terrain is less steep, making for an easier path. Enter the woods on the second point in from the main lake. Follow the ridgeline straight up. Soon you will see a towering castle of rock near the top. That is the famed hideout for our Spaniards that met their demise. Before you reach that rocky tower, the Great Beech will be standing on your right. You won't miss it. Pause here and say a little prayer for old GW.

To find the Spanish Diggings, veer right after the Great Beech and cross the ravine. Three levels of dozer paths have flattened the terrain there. Another huge lone Beech tree stands there also, guarding this old treasure trove of history. It's gotten many initials carved into it over the years also. Treat both these trees with respect. They have seen many of us come and go. Let's hope they meet our grandchildren.

And that's my treasure story, folks. I wrote a whole book on this old tale. It's called "Lost Treasure". And even though I am certain no treasure will ever be dug there, I just love that old story. In my research for this tale, I have met new friends and reaffirmed old ones. I've learned the rich history that old trail has to offer. And in that…I believe I've found the treasure. ~

Spanish Trail Map

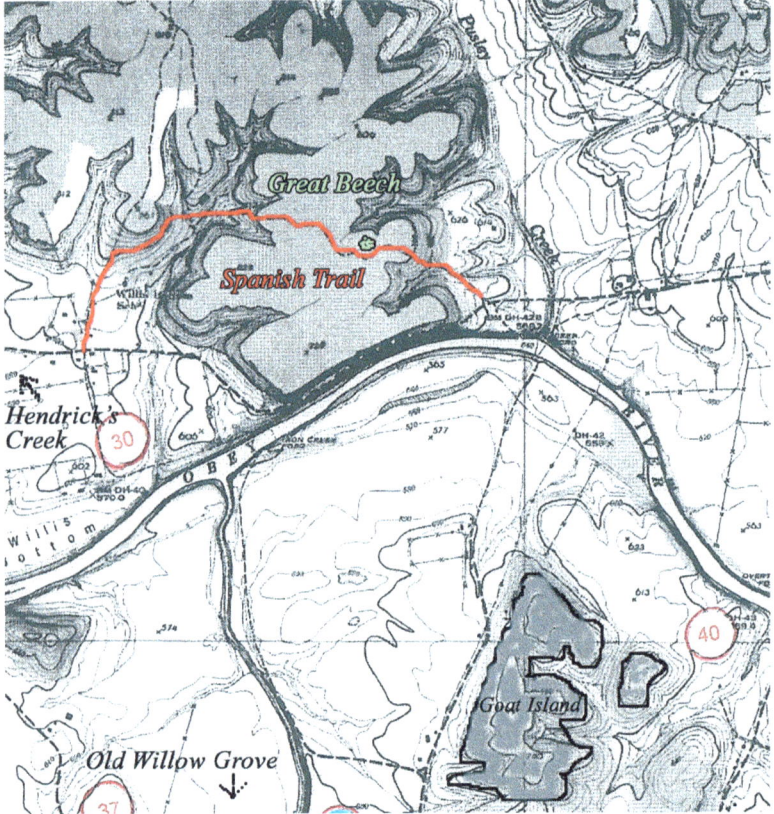

The Great Beech Tree
G. W. Sevier, Jr.
March 15
1899

Throwing Stones

Lake Times News, November, 2007
Darren Shell

Mother always told me, "You shouldn't throw stones...you'll break something!" And she was right. 'Course, I was never much of an aim. I don't suppose my lack of ability and accuracy helped, but lately I've had a slight change in my thinking process when it comes to the tossing of rocks. It seems I've met a *rock-solid* family here on Dale Hollow. And we might all learn a thing or two from this bunch. We just have to think beyond what we most consider as the "norm".

My story starts with the low water. As most of us lake-lovers know, our beautiful lake has dropped its level to a staggeringly shallow depth. In this inevitable process, most of us boat dock boys have found ourselves shuffling slips and moving docks to new and unheard-of locations. We all have dirt and mud where our lavish blanket of clear water once provided ample depth for our many boats. It was at this low water level where I saw something I hadn't noticed before.

On one of my recent dock-moving walks along shore, I noticed something that made me smile. What I saw not only made me smile...it made me laugh out loud. Still smiling, a tear slid down my nose, as a whole lot of recent memories started flowing through my head. It went something like this...

A few years ago, a family moved their houseboat to my marina. Chris and Anita brought their houseboat and their two children, Lance and Morgan, to our slips and quickly became fast friends with nearly everyone on their dock. It is wonderful how the pastime of house boating brings a family together and somehow keeps them together. It is a fantastic means of relaxation that seems to draw families and friends near. It provides a rich and rewarding connection to nature that few other pastimes can present. This family has drawn from that energy and has taken it to yet another level.

This family, in many ways, is special. Like many other families in the area, they love the lake. I mean…they LOVE it. They make every attempt to "make the lake" every warm weekend in summer. Kudos to them! But it is difficult for this family to enjoy the lake like the most of us. They have one obstacle that sometimes presents a problem. They have one difficulty that is both challenging…and rewarding at the same time. The Robinson's son, Lance has autism. At age 13, Lance is strong and healthy, and very much in tune with life. And although he has his rough days, Lance spends many hours on our shores, enjoying himself in one of the few ways he knows how.

Lance throws rocks.

He doesn't just toss a few stones into the lake. He throws rocks…and he throws them nearly all day. He'll take a break from his pitching to eat lunch, or perhaps enjoy a reward of Skittles and Mt. Dew from the marina. But then, it's back to the serious lake business of throwing rocks. From the early wee morning hours, to the post-dark times of late evening…Lance throws rocks. Little ones…small ones…ones good for skipping. They are all worthy of a nice splash. And those splashes happen often and constant.

Even though this boating family chooses to spend most of their time out in one of Dale Hollow's great coves, they sometimes spend a few evenings here in the Willow Grove hollow. And that's just fine. Lance can walk the shore…in complete view of his family…and do what he does best. He throws rocks. He will walk the shore between his dock and the main ship store and toss stones into the lake, loving that exciting splash of water. There just must be something in that splash…that's all I can say. The full length of that stretch of shore has been fully covered by Lance…in his ever-increasing joy of throwing rocks. We have often joked… "Maybe we need to have a load of rocks dumped there for him…Lance is running out of "Good" rocks!" His enthusiastic joy of tossing stones has touched us all. Lance doesn't always acknowledge us when we chat playfully with him about his passion for tossing rocks, but his enthusiasm is contagious. We are all inspired by this family's perseverance, and Lance's passion for this lake he loves. It has been a release for the family as a whole. It is definitely difficult for this family to "boat" under this special condition, but they have pressed forward with a grace and love of *Family*. And I think we could all use a good dose of that.

Lance Robinson, Spring 2008

So, quite frankly, this is what I wanted to share with you lake-loving folks out there. Willow Grove has set out on a mission. We have a job to do before the lake rises. It seems that the upper portion of the banks of my hollow are hopelessly devoid of rocks. There is just nothing left to throw. The lower levels have COUNTLESS volumes of "thrown" rocks resting on its lower muddy shores. They're all over the place! I'm not kidding, folks.

I had no idea of the true volume of Lance's endeavors, until that one dock-moving day after the lake level dropped and I saw what remained from years of rock-throwing fun enjoyed by Lance. That was the day when I smiled and laughed and reflected upon this special Lake-Family. Thousands of rocks now lie on this one hundred yard stretch of bank between Lance's dock and the Skittle-getting-place-marina. The low water table has revealed years of Lance's work.

So here's my challenge. There's only one Lance...but hundreds of us. What if...what if...we put them all back? I'm talking about tons of rocks. Thousands of stones. I mean rock after rock after rock...all right there on shore. What do you say...let's throw them all back. Why not toss a few stones up hill? Mom always told me not to throw stones...but this might be an exception to the rule!

Lance lives his life in a place where all can see him. He is under our constant gaze. His boating family is always on a vigilant watch as he paces the shoreline. One could definitely say that Lance lives in a glass house. But despite the old adage...I think perhaps...our friend, Lance, *should* always throw stones...and I'll be standing here willing to throw them back. ~

Lance's Thrown Stones, Fall, 2007

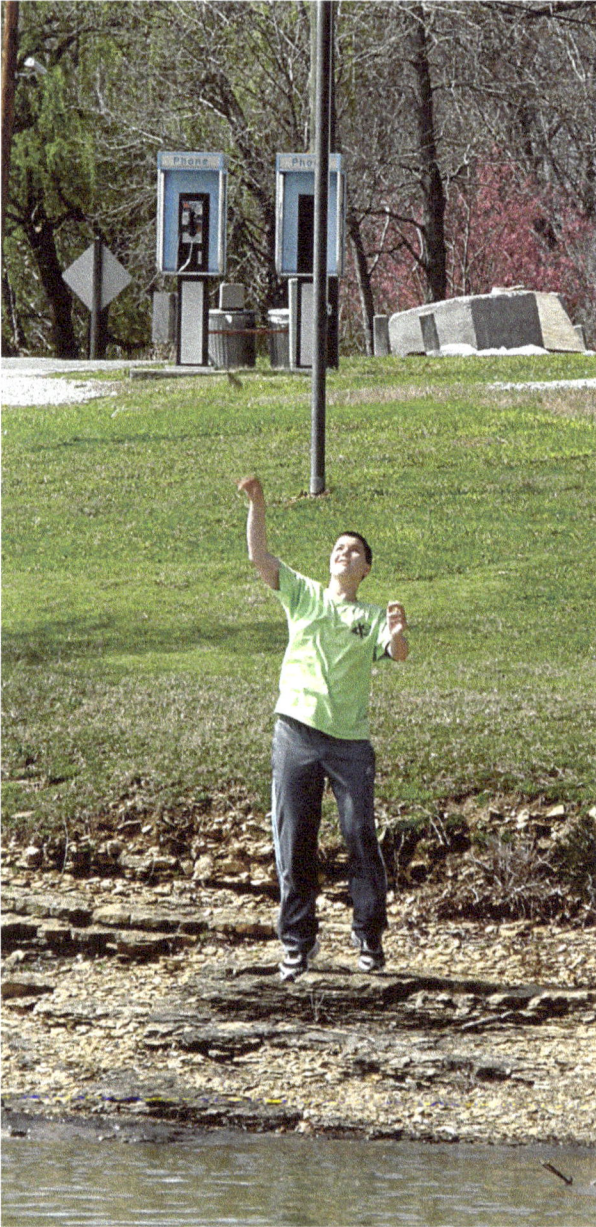

Lance Robinson, Spring, 2008
Photo courtesy of Gerald and Cindy Craycraft

Ode to an Old Guide

I've always been sort of a low-tech kinda guy. In   fact, I can barely manage to type out my stories in a computer format suitable for use in this decade. That being said, I'd like to share a low-tech fishing story with you about a friend of mine that lived a short while back. He was a fishing guide on Dale Hollow for decades, back when GPS devices and multi-thousand-dollar digital equipment took over the fishing arena. This was a time before the term bass-boat made sense to anyone. This was a time when fishing was more about the man and less about the machine. This story is about my first fishing trip with a man from Livingston, Tennessee, known by thousands of savvy fishermen. Let me tell you about Tommy Gray.

I was fourteen years old and no bigger than the little end of nothin'. I stood bewildered on the edge of the pier at my family marina as two men pulled smallmouth bass from a trash can full of ice. I stood almost trembling as I counted, "One, two, three…". My tongue got tired before they were through lifting these beautiful golden beauties from the boat. They hooked them all on a steel rack that showed them off in all their glory. That's the way they did it back then. No size limits, no creel limits, no catch and release of any form. In this day and age, shock and horror would take place. In those days…those men were Gods.

"Who's that, Dad?" I asked quietly, so as not to cause a stir.

"Oh, that's Tommy and John Tom from Livingston. Looks like they had a good night."

"A good night?" I exclaimed. "I think the heavens opened and rained fish for them." Dad just smiled and patted me on the shoulder. To my surprise, the bigger of the two men must have overheard me and made his way over near me. He leaned down to my eye level and gave me a long stare. His wide grin was wrapped around a stub of a cigar tucked over into one side of his mouth.

"Tom Gray's the name, Boy…You?" His grin continued as he stuck out his fishy hand. I quickly reached out mine and took hold. My little hand disappeared into his calloused and clammy palm.

"Darren…I mean, Darren, Sir."

"Stop with the Sir, Boy. I ain't cha Daddy." He gave my father a wry wink. "You look like a fisherman, I'd say. Wanna go some night?"

I know my head was nodding like a bobble-headed dog. ""Uh, uh, umhum." That was the best yes I could muster.

And that's how I ended up in the boat with local fishing guide, Tommy Gray. Looking back, that was pretty impressive for someone in his position to notice the snot-nosed little kid off to the side. It made an impression on me then, and even more so now. He didn't have to do that.

A night or two later, I found myself on the dock in the near darkness. The moon was almost full, but the clouds were shadowing the sparkles on the water. It was a calm night, and I sat perfectly still taking in all I could before we embarked on this special trip. I knew Old Tommy didn't need me in the boat; he was just being kind hearted enough to show the little rookie what smallmouth fishing was all about. I wanted to learn the shrewd and cunning ways of a true fisherman, and that night I certainly did. And he did it all with about $20 worth of gear. I was amazed.

I stepped into the boat and sat down, staring at the simplicity of the boat. It was a simple tri-hull with no trolling motor, no live well, and no depth finder of any sort (or so I thought). There were just two rods, a bucket, and a small tackle box. "That one will be yours," he said, motioning toward one of the rods. "Now when we stop, be ready to anchor."

Again I scanned the boat, seeing nothing of the sort. "It's in the bucket, Boy." The whole time I knew him, he never spoke my name, but it never bothered me in the slightest.

I slid the bucket near and rummaged through its contents. One thin rope, one concrete anchor made from a coffee can, and nothing else. I soon found out that this high-tech system was his anchoring and navigating system. The rope was tied to the bucket on one end and the anchor on the other. If he wanted the boat to drift slowly in a wind, he'd instruct me to leave the anchor in the boat and toss over the bucket. The bucket acted like a small parachute, slowing the boat. Plus, one could place the anchor in the front or back of the boat, depending on how you wanted the boat to face. And of course, there were times I'd leave the bucket in the boat (full of water) and toss the anchor overboard, thus halting the craft altogether, with the same placement of the bucket to control the boat's angle to the wind.

All this from a bucket, string, and anchor. Forrest Wood, eat your heart out.

By now, we are top speed, flying through the Dale Hollow darkness. I'm about to pee my pants, alright. I have no idea where we are or if there is a giant rock wall about to jump out in front of us, or if the rock bottom will soon jettison us into the night sky. I was so tickled to hear the engine slow its rpm, but it didn't have the chance to slow to idle. To my surprise, Tom reached over and turned off the key. Before the boat had even settled into the water, he took three steps to the front of the boat, grabbing his pole on the way. Two more seconds pass and he has cast deep into the night sky. Ker-plop, I hear his bait drop into the Dale. I hear him grunt past his cigar. "Bucket."

"What?" I asked sheepishly.

He rapped off a string of obscenities with the word bucket attached near the end. I raced to the bucket and tossed it in. In a matter of seconds, the rope was snug and our pace had slowed. I turned and reached for my pole, but had no time to pick it up. I heard and felt Tom tug for all he was worth on his pole. It met tension immediately and doubled over with the fish on the other end of the line. "Net, Boy!" he exclaimed.

I did manage to find a small dip net under the helm. It looked like one of the trout nets they use on the river. Heck, I could stick it in my pocket if I wanted. After a minute or two, Tom tugged the fish near the boat and I dipped it quickly from the lake. It was a pretty thing, probably four pounds of golden, shiny smallmouth. "Anchor, Boy." As Tom tossed the fish into a compartment in the front of the boat, I furiously tugged in the bucket and tossed in the anchor. I turned and reached for my pole. Nope.

"How deep is it, Boy?" I know I had a stupid look on my face, but thankfully the darkness hid some of it. Before I knew it, he had dug into his pocket and tossed me a handful of something. It was a string tied to a washer, and the string was all different colors. "Drop it over," he said.

So I did. I felt it touch the bottom. He saw the line go slack and asked, "What color is it?" I shined my little flashlight at the surface of the water where the line entered.

"Red," I answered.

"Good," he replied. "Twenty feet."

As I retrieved the line and washer from the lake, I noticed the string changing colors. This old guy had memorized a series of colors up this line and knew what depth we were sitting in. That's high tech.

Bang. He's got another. "Net, boy." I dipped a fine three pounder, and he tossed it into his compartment. I reach for my pole reluctantly, eyeing him for approval. "Are you gonna fish or just play in the boat?"

I smiled. I knew he was joking. I made one cast in the same basic direction as him. I felt the mossy bottom dragging at my lure. "Crank a little faster, Boy." I did, of course. Bang. My pole nearly ejected from my hands as it bent under pressure. Tom shouted all sorts of commands at me as I cranked in my first four pound smallmouth ever. "Rod tip up, Boy. Don't force it. Loosen the drag." I finally pull it near the boat, and Tom thumbs the fish in the bottom lip, dragging it into the boat. Pretty! He tosses it into his compartment and I prepare to cast. "Bucket, Boy."

Dang. Maybe he did need me after all.

Well, that was twenty-five years ago, folks. Now my bass boat has more gadgets than I know how to use, and I still can't find that magical spot out there in the darkness of Dale Hollow I fished so many years ago with Tommy. Old Tom is no longer with us, but his fishing experience is still right where it's always been … tucked away in a little corner of my heart, where low-tech methods are still used by high-tech kind of guides. Guides like my friend, Tommy Gray.

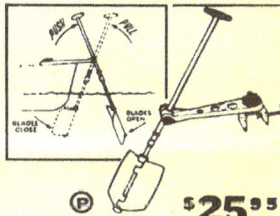

Map Advertisement, 1968

FISHERMAN & CAMPER GUIDE
Price $1.50
Guide Map to Better Fishing and Camping
DALE HOLLOW
Recommended by Tommy Gray, Guide
Phone TA 3-6177 – Livingston, Tenn.

Dale Hollow—the home of the lunker bass. This lake holds the world record on small mouth—11 lb. 15 oz. Dock operators and guides around the lake say they are looking for a big year on bass and other game fish in '68.

DALE HOLLOW.............provides some of the best fishing anywhere. But if you don't know the lake, or hire a guide who does, you may spend more time hunting for fish than catching any. This map lets you fish as if you had an army of the best guides at your side.

It is based on information and personal fishing trips with some of the better guides on this lake. They have marked the spots that are best for bass, crappie, and walleye. You'll see some of their catches pictured inside, along with details concerning lures used and the best time for fishing the lake.

Refer to the map often – just as you would a guide – to lead you to successful fishing.

D & D Maps Corp.   © Copyright 1968

Map marked by guide, Tommy Gray, 1968
Entire map is available in digital format from the author.

154

An Amphibious Journey From Star Point to Lillydale Campground

Few of us that ski and swim and play near Jouett Creek realize what once rested beneath the waves of our favorite coves and points in the middle of Dale Hollow. The natural terrain around us now shows us little of what was once a thriving little community full of hustle and bustle of 1930s life. Few now know about Old Hwy 53 between Star Point and Lillydale Campground. It once connected the town of Willow Grove to the city of Byrdstown, via the communities of Lillydale and Star Point. It was the largest and best maintained stretch of road within miles. It had a great asphalt surface and numerous culverts to manage run-off water from the mountainous terrain. It was THE highway around here, and countless individuals graced its surface over the years. I'd like to take you on a quick drive from Star Point over to Lillydale Campground, both in the present and in the past.. What we might see may surprise you.

Star Point Boat Ramp, Spring, 2008

Alrighty folks, here we sit on the Star Point boat ramp. We've got the engine running, and the waves are gently slapping at the shore in front of us. It's hard to picture this hollow without all this water, and even tougher to see the old road ahead of us. But that old road is still there, leading us onward to Lillydale. We just gotta take the plunge. So buckle up and take a deep breath. We're going in. Got your window shut tight?

Well, this isn't so bad. Our automobile/time machine is rolling along just fine. On this journey, we can see both the past and the present. There are colorful sights and sounds around us, and black-and-white visions of yesteryear within our view also. This is one weird ride. Let's take a look around.

As we roll along out of Jouett Creek, the road barely turns at all. It stretches out in front of us, inching its way westward. Just look at all those propellers turning above us. There are all sorts of activities taking place above our heads as we drive…boats are speeding along, skiers are dashing side to side, and the splashes of children playing in the water echo down to our depth. There is just so much energy here.

Even though the cove bends to the left and meets the main lake, our road still leads us nearly straight ahead. And now we are going uphill. Those propellers are getting closer. You keep an eye on those props as I drive up onto shore. This looks like a neat place. I think we should get out and look around.

We are now on the Jouett Creek point. We've made our way through the trees just like they weren't even there. The old road bed is still just as flat as the day it was fashioned. Look at these awesome culverts still in the ground. There must be four or five of them, still fulfilling their job created over 65 years ago. We could crawl through them if we wished, but they look a little creepy. And look at this asphalt. It looks like the common chip-and-seal roadwork still used today. It's still here too, and so few folks ever see it. In fact, it's crumbling off and falling into the water right behind the Jouett Creek sign. The sign itself is pushed into the old road, now directing boats instead of cars.

Sheryl Shell, Hwy 53 culvert at Jouett Creek, Spring, 2008

Lauren Shell, Hwy 53 Road Bed, Winter, 2006

But there is much more here on this point. This little stop-off on our trip has landed us in a special location. I'm starting to see the black and white. As we stand on the old road, near our old culverts, we can look south, toward Ashburn Creek. County Line Island is just visible through the dense trees. I see both colors. In black and white, it is called The Martha Knob. In color…County Line Island. I see old man Arney tending the large cemetery on the point of the island and also the dirt road leading through the cut into Ashburn. Someday we may take that road too, but we'll stay on Hwy 53 today.

As I stare out at the Martha Knob, I am distracted by a bunch of black and white stones between me and the beautiful green water. Let's step off the road and walk toward the water. As I walk down hill, I can clearly see tall granite markers. There are many rows of them. This is the Jouett Cemetery. Thirty-nine graves were removed from this spot when the lake was created.

Some were moved to the Lillydale area and others to Byrdstown. Their large vacant holes are still here in color.

No. 69: Jouett #1 Cemetery

Jouett Cemetery, 1942

But what's this? Even before we reach the wonderfully-carved headstones in the distance, there are rows of tiny stones here too, right near the road. These are merely minute fieldstones with no markings. They are just a few rows of sunken holes and tiny rock reminders of a small African-American community just east of here. They were part of the community known as Lower Harrison. And these twenty-six poor souls didn't get moved nearby. They, like all the black graveyards on Corps property, were moved north of Celina, Tennessee, to a community called Free Hills. Strange, though. In color, there are many large holes in the soil down by the water. Up here, I see no sunken holes from grave removal. Kinda makes me wonder if these black folk souls might still be here, with only their stones removed. Maybe they are here in color too.

No. 68: Jouett #2 Cemetery

African American Gravesite, Jouett Creek, 1942

Before we leave, I'd like to show you one more thing (no graves, I promise!). Let's walk beyond the cemeteries and out to the edge of the lake. Out on this point is a pile of large stones. They are nicely carved rocks all jumbled up into a pile. When the water is down, we can walk around them and imagine what they might have been. Right now, with the colorful water washing over them, we can only imagine them some fifty feet off shore. These historical rocks were the Lower Harrison School House. This large clapboard building once adorned this point overlooking the lazy Obey River, as it wound its way toward its juncture with the Wolf. Those rocks still stand as a testament to the sturdy individuals that were educated there. It's a wonderful view too, both in color and in black and white.

But let's jump back in the car. I've saved the best for last.

Let's cruise past the Jouett Creek sign and reenter the lake. It feels creepy submerging again into the dark depths of the Dale. Let's focus on the black and white. We can now plainly see the houses and buildings of Lillydale to our right. I hear the church bell ringing in the distance. A few houses dot the old Obey's shores to our left, part of Martha's Knob. And in color, I can see the shores of present day Lillydale Campground, although those pesky propellers keep churning up the view. This has always been a busy place, in color and in black and white.

But now we are stopped in the dead center of the lake. We can see the juncture of the Wolf and the Obey to our right. We can see the church house and the kids playing there in black and white. There are farm fields all around us, with cattle grazing and tufts of corn tassels blowing in the slight breeze. But I've stopped here for a reason. I'm a little nervous. The Obey River is between us and Lillydale Campground. The only way across...is this massive bridge. I've never driven across it. Parts of it are so high that they reach color in the black and white desolation of Dale Hollow's murky depths. The large framework trellis must stretch some one hundred yards before reaching the huge steel arches. Wow, that's a long way up.

Lillydale Bridge, late 1930s

We might as well do it. Let's roll forward. Despite the narrow crossing provided for us, this is quite a strong bridge. It was only built just a few years prior to its dismantling to build the lake. It only carried a few years' worth of people across the Obey, but what an awesome sight! From our high perch, we can see far upstream and far up into the Wolf. The houses on the Lillydale point are now coming into view. As we reach the far shore, the road makes a sharp left and now everything is in color again.

Lillydale Gatehouse

Campsites dot the shore. Bathhouses are here and there. A gatehouse sets in the middle of the road. I guess we've completed our mission. We could travel on to Willow Grove on this same road, but that just might be a journey for another day. I think maybe I'll just turn around. Sometimes I like the black and white scenery around here. Maybe I'll go back and help old man Arney clean the cemetery. The sky is a lovely shade of gray, and the birds of yesteryear are chirping. The tall grasses in the field are swaying in tones of off-white and black. That old gray bridge is calling my name. And life on old Hwy 53 is grand. ~

A View From the Plankyard

Byrdstown, Tennessee

Every now and then, I drop my old 1958 Lyman runabout off the lift and go float around someplace on the Dale and study my old maps. It's amazing what you can see as you drift along while the gentle lapping waves tap on the side of the boat. If you use your imagination, you can see this place as it was, some sixty-five years ago. In my mind, I can see the old roads and buildings. I can picture the forgotten cemeteries beneath the waves. I can just feel the history pulsating beneath me.

Let's motor up to Byrdstown and check things out, shall we?

I reach over and shut off the ignition. The old Lyman glides on through the waves near Sunset Marina as drops of Dale Hollow dry on its mahogany bow. The warm sun feels great on my back, and I can't resist a quick dip in the lake. Ahhhh! Don't get no better 'n Dale Hollow.

Today, I'm floating near the water plant, just outside of the no ski zone in front of Obey River Campground. Seems like an unassuming place, I must say. It's just a big open body of water where the city of Byrdstown draws its water with this giant steel pier along shore. This northern bank has a twisted, narrow little road carved into its face. This old road looks like nothing but a nearly forgotten logging trail, but it was once so much more. It's hard to believe that sixty-five years ago that this was the most heavily traveled road in Pickett County. Hundreds and hundreds of vehicles traversed this crude path up the mountain. Right where we float, right in front of this nicely built water-pumping structure, once stood the Obey River Bridge. And she was a beauty.

First Obey River Bridge on Hwy 42
Byrdstown, Tennessee
Built 1917

Obey River Ferry on Hwy 42, Byrdstown

Both Bridges over Sunset Marina
Photo courtesy of Johnnie Hugh, ©1996

It's hard to imagine this giant body of water as only a narrow river. The bridge that crossed this river was enormous in its day, even though the colossal bridge we now see would have dwarfed it by immeasurable means. It started out as a ferry and then became the concrete statue that most considered the greatest structure of its day. It connected the town of Byrdstown to its sister city, Livingston, Tennessee. Old Hwy 42 wound down through the campground and crossed the river to the northern shore. On this north bank sat The Plankyard. It was a logging stop along the river for years, and became known as The Plankyard for its numerous wood sawing ventures for the city of Byrdstown. Even to this day, local boaters still launch their boats where their ancestors did…at The Plankyard.

Let's look around and see what else we can see.

What is now the campground, was once a fantastic natural pasture. Native American Indians first farmed these shores long before we Americans took a liking to them. This long riverside farming community eventually became home to many families here in the valley. Parrises and Copes, Warrens and Robbins all lived here…and died here. Three different cemeteries were moved from these acres before the lake was flooded. Parris Island still shows signs of its long-ago graveyard. Most of these souls were moved to the Cope Cemetery in Byrdstown, hopefully disrupted for the last time.

Let's see…what else. Look far, far upstream. Just at the bend of the river beyond the marina was a tiny community uncommonly known as Winningham. No, it's not on any maps. It's not documented anywhere, really. But it is where a family of African Americans had created their homestead. Black folk were few back in those days, and this little section of river was but a tiny little settlement of a handful of logging men and their families. The logging men of the day worked the hard and dangerous Obey River to feed their families. They too had their own cemeteries along the river. Their graves were supposedly moved as well. Shame, though…not one African American name was documented during the grave removals to build the lake. Not one. Unfortunately, many of the blacks had little money for official headstones, and of course, those were different days, decades ago. The world is different now. So, even though the Corps never named the black cemeteries, I choose to call these little graveyards by their names. The first is the Winningham Cemetery (13 graves moved). The next one upstream is the Byrd Cemetery (2 graves, husband and wife). All African American *Unknowns* were reentered at Free Hill Cemetery in Celina, where every black person was removed to. They are no longer where they wanted to be. They are all piled up together in Celina, Tennessee…along with their kindred.

There is another tidbit of interesting history viewable from here. If we look downstream, just behind the campground, we will notice the high bluff that overlooks the lake. It is now a series of subdivisions full of houses. But it was once home to this area's very first settlers. Few realize that on the point overlooking Eagle Creek, high up on the bluff, is the cemetery known as Keisling/Knight Cemetery. The main reason I mention it is because of its residents. I don't like to talk about graves all the time, but those buried in this cemetery lived in a time nothing like what we know as normal. These people helped forge this country…not just Tennessee, but this country. In this tiny graveyard over Dale Hollow, veterans from four different wars are buried. And I'm not talking about recent history, people. I'm talking true founding Americans. Those who lived and died for this country long before this country's sense of entitlement has gotten so out-of-whack.

In this precious piece of real-estate, there are veterans from the Revolutionary War, War of 1812, Civil War, and one as recent as the war with Korea. With a cemetery with so little as 27 interments, to have veterans of four wars is noteworthy...it's amazing really. I canvassed the headstones in 2006. It was a moving experience for me.

But I think its time I awaken from this daydream. My boat has nearly drifted ashore. I'm sure I'm sunburned. And you know...I'm hungry. I'll bet Sunset's got nachos with my name on them. I'll bet I can make those nachos...*history!* Or I'm not the Gravedigger. ~

Obey River Ferry, Early 1900s
Photo Courtesy of Elaine Pennington
Livingston, Tennessee

Unknown Motorists Crossing the Obey River Bridge, about 1920
Photo Courtesy of Elaine Pennington, Livingston, TN

A View from Wolf River Marina

There was a time, long ago, when the road to Wolf River Marina was actually the road from Albany, Kentucky, to a small community known as Miller's Mill. Most of this little village existed just beyond the idle buoys. Why don't we sit ourselves down on the end of the houseboat dock pier and see what we can see. Let's grab a bag of chips and a cold soda pop from the ship's store and have a look around. I'll bet there's more here than meets the eye.

Authors at Wolf River Marina, Spring, 2008

As you might have guessed, Miller's Mill did actually have a mill on the Wolf River right out in front of us. On the point at the bend of the river in front of us sat a clapboard building full of turning wheels and gears that ground corn and wheat and many other necessities for farming life. The currents of the Wolf powered this wonderful old building, its waters ever pushing at that large spinning wheel of wood and water that forced life into this machine/building. Its constant churning motions breathed life into this tiny community. Farmers and families all along the river utilized this mainstay business along the Wolf. It was commerce-central, and everyone nearby used the mill for their family needs. Mr. Dallas Little operated the mill and store from the 1920s on up until the Corps purchased his property to build the lake. Prior to him, Mr. Samuel Phillips ran the Mill for a number of years in the late 1800s.

Miller's Mill House, early 1900s

Miller's Mill Dam, 1940, O. S. Coop and daughter, Nancy
Photo Courtesy of Elaine Pennington, Livingston, TN

If we look just a little to the left, just before the mouth of Sewell Creek, we can easily see (beneath the waves) the old church. Miller's Chapel rested along the bluff right near the old road that edged along the far side of the river. We could toss a rock from the church's front porch and hear the splash in the mighty Wolf. I can almost hear the rippling currents of the Wolf as the old church bell echoes through the hills. Children in their Sunday-best are scampering through the yard. What a lovely place.

If we step out into the backyard of the church, we can now see the headstones of the Miller's Chapel Cemetery. Eighteen souls were removed from here in 1941/42 and carted up to Amonett Cemetery in Byrdstown. Many of our Pickett County lake graves were moved to this giant cemetery along the Star Point road.

Millers Chapel Dis.

No. 100: Miller's Chapel #2 Cemetery

Let's take a little broader view. Imagine every acre of land to our left. Imagine hundreds of acres of farmland along the river upstream. Two miles of this river was once deeded to this area's first white settler. Mr. James Harrison, a Revolutionary War

173

veteran, owned the vast majority of this wonderful stretch of river from here on upstream. During most of the 1800s, this man and his family farmed the river valley and called it home. When the property finally changed hands in the late 1800s, it was purchased (oddly enough) by another war veteran, Mr. Granville Groce, a Civil War soldier. His family mapped it out and gave it a title. It was known as Duck Head Farm, named because of the odd duck head shape the river had carved at what we call Sheer Pin Pass. If we study the lake map, the river does create an odd duck head shape there at the bend of the river. And this great farmland took a name for itself. The Groce family was the last to farm this stretch of river. The last change of hands of this property resulted in the building of Dale Hollow Lake. A large portion of the Duck Head Farm is now under Corps ownership. Most of the developed subdivisions around Sheer Pin were once Duck Head Farm property. And the world turns.

Miller's Mill Store, 1940

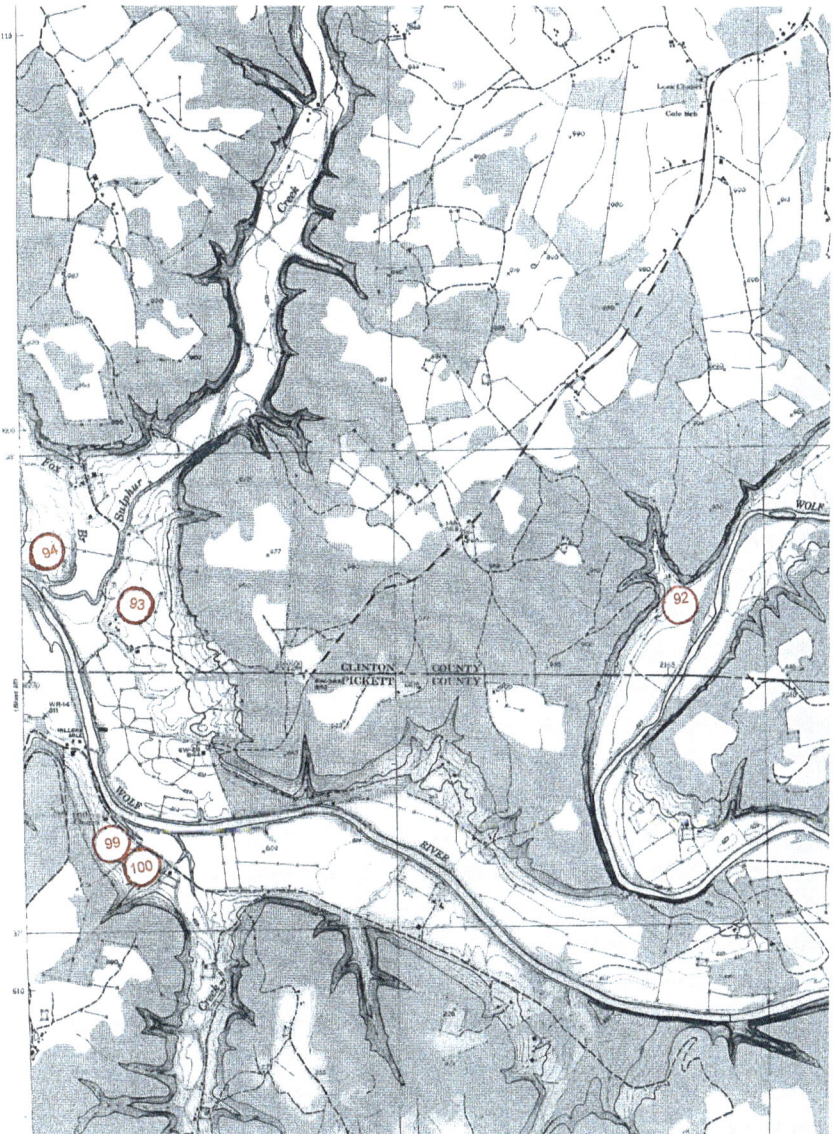

Red Circles Denote Disinterred Cemeteries

I'd also like to mention the community of Jones Chapel. If we look to the left of Sewell Creek, we can still catch a glimpse of the old road that enters the water at Meeting House Branch. That was our Albany Road, if you will. Some maps show the community of Jones Chapel near the water; others show it where it is now, high on the hill. This community still has fantastic cemeteries full of important people we should all know about. But that's another history story waiting to be told. I'll tell that one another day.

Well, my bag of chips is empty and my Pepsi Cola is gone. I guess we'd better wrap this up. But I have one more topic to discuss with you. This is the one that creeps everybody out. Most of you know by now that I have studied and mapped all the old cemeteries of Dale Hollow Lake. Some say I love to creep people out with death and graves. But really I don't. I just think that a burial site should be respected, especially if we don't know for certain what is still contained there. I've been to all of the old Corps-removed cemeteries above water. I know, without question, if the graves were actually moved or just "sort-of" moved. But what of the ones under water that we can't see? How can we be sure what resides there?

That being said, let me tell you about the graveyard directly under us...right under this set of boat slips. It's the L.C. Cummins Cemetery. Twenty-eight souls were disinterred here. Or were they? We can't see the deeply dug holes of removed graves. We can't see the small depressions of unmoved graves. All we have is a sunken cemetery. And that's how it will always be. We'll probably never know if those folks are still there.

Part of me wishes that those folks were removed from the dark and murky depths of Dale Hollow. And another part of me hopes they are still residing where they wanted to rest...where the old mill still churns and the church bell still rings. Warm fields of hay still wave in the light river breeze. It's a beautiful place. I can see it all before us...and right below us. If those twenty-eight souls still share our view, then so be it. It's an awesome view we have here from the boat slips. The mill still grinds, the church still offers comfort, and hundreds of boaters ski and play in the wonderful waters of the Wolf. And the world still turns here on the Duck Head farm of Wolf River. ~

Painting of Miller's Mill by Evelyn Cummings
Miller's Chapel Church in the Distance

Frank's Hard Day

Some say Frank was having a bad day. Others said he must have been having a superb day since he lived through it and all. But one thing's for certain, he wasn't having an ordinary day in the town of old Willow Grove. And it all started with his tummy-ache.

Frank Sevier rolled over in bed. It still wasn't quite daylight yet, but the churning in his stomach had kept him restless all night, and it was only getting worse. He finally crawled out of his old feather-tick bed and wandered out to the kitchen table.

He nibbled at a leftover biscuit, trying to find something to ease the pain down low in his abdomen. Nothing helped. When daylight finally rolled around, he was already walking (stumbling) into town. He had to do something. He soon found himself entering Virgil Grimsley's store.

Virgil's little store carried about everything, and it was the closest thing to a pharmacy that this country town had to offer. Frank hoped to find something on the shelf to help ease his suffering. Shoot, anything to make this pain go away. But Frank was in luck, or so it seemed. As was common practice, Willow Grove's two local doctors were starting their day at Virgil's store and stocking up on meds before making their rounds through the community. Dr. Edward Clark and Dr. Walter Sidwell were chatting as Frank entered.

"You look awful, Frank," they exclaimed, as they eased him into a chair for an evaluation. In a matter of seconds, both doctors recognized the symptoms of appendicitis. If something wasn't done soon, Frank's appendix could rupture, and he could die right here in the store. Both doctors were hesitant to let Frank in on their conclusion.

"Hop up here, Frank," Doc Clark suggested, pointing toward the grocery counter. "Virgil is going to put some medicine on a cloth and hold it near your nose. The smell of the stuff should help ease your pain."

Frank looked uncertain. "Gosh, Doc...that stuff smells awful."

"Yeah, Frank," commented Dr. Sidwell, "but it'll make some of the pain go away."

Frank did as he was told, taking in breaths of chloroform fumes. It eased his suffering, alright. It knocked him out cold. "Nice job," said Doc, smiling at Virgil. "That should just about do it."

Well, you can imagine what happened next. Two doctors washed up, as Virgil cleaned the skin of Frank's stomach and waist. And as the town of Willow Grove shopped for their morning groceries in Virgil's little store, Frank Sevier received an appendectomy right on the check out counter. No kidding.

All of this seems unfathomable in this day and time, when lavish hospitals grace every city. But back in the 1920s and 30s, old Willow Grove didn't have that luxury. The small hospital in Livingston was twenty miles away, and Frank was in no condition for travel. So these two savvy doctors took the bull by the horns and made the harsh decision. Frank's life was on the line. That appendix had to come out, and fast. In a matter of only a minute or two, Dr. Sidwell had made a small incision in Frank's stomach and eased his appendix out of his body. Doc Clark made a couple of quick stitches, and with quick snip of his scissors, Frank's appendix was quickly dropped into a jar. Another few stitches sewed Frank back together, and a quick application of bag balm salve offered a finishing touch to the procedure. And Frank was good as new.

Well, almost. As the last dabbing of salve was being applied, Frank came-to with a growl of discomfort. "God, Doc," exclaimed Frank, "I think I've been shot."

"Naw, Frank," commented Virgil, "just a little minor surgery."

"You cut me open?" Frank could hardly believe his ears.

The three men smiled…and so did a half dozen shoppers ready to check out.

"Let's walk you home, Frank," said Doc.

Walk him home? The guy just had his appendix yanked out, and they were gonna walk him home? Well, that's just what they did. After an emergency appendectomy on the check out counter of his local country store, Frank Sevier walked home. I've had my appendix removed, Folks, and I didn't walk home. I didn't walk for three days. I guess people were just tougher back in those days.

I think about old Frank now and then when I'm at my general store. When I'm checking out at Wal-Mart, I sometimes look over at the pharmacy and wonder if there is a Dr. Sidwell or Doc Clark standing around in case I need emergency surgery. I wonder if my credit card limit would cover the surgery. And I wonder if this cashier will know where to scan me for an appendectomy bar code. With any luck, maybe there's a bag boy that will throw me in a shopping cart afterward and dump me at my truck. I'd be good as new…almost.

So think about old Frank as you ski and play over this wonderful body of water called Dale Hollow. If you fall and break a leg, there will probably be a chopper land nearby and whisk you away to Vanderbilt Hospital a hundred miles away. Or…we could just flop you up on the counter and grab the bag balm. Shoot, I'd even walk you home. ~

Dr. Walter F. Sidwell, early 1900s

The Cherokee Nation

So many lake lovers come and go, and they never get the opportunity to see and feel some of our rich heritage. When the sunburns fade, and the family car is unloaded from its long vacation travels, few ponder those that walked before us in these hills and hollows of Tennessee and Kentucky. Those true Americans from so very long ago lived a rich life along our streams and waterfalls and caves near this body of water. Native Americans called these shores home centuries longer than we immigrants that now claim ownership. Let me tell you about one such group. Let's talk about the Cherokee.

Now, historians across these two fine states often argue over which tribes were here first and last, as well as those that intermingled throughout society as they knew it. I don't intend to claim vast knowledge about the specifics of any of these tribes of our area. There were countless Native Americans that both lived and traveled through this rich valley. Volumes of lavish books have been written on the subject, so I won't delve to that depth. But I think the world should know a little about our Cherokee tribe that last lived here on the banks of the Obey River (then known as the Obed).

Chief Nettlecarrier was considered by most as the *Last Great Cherokee Chief of the Obey River Valley.* Of course, he was known far and wide from the upper waters of the East and West Forks of the Obey River, to the counties south of this winding body of water. Other well-known names in that tribe were

Chief Obed (quite possibly Nettlecarrier's father, or at least a predecessor. It is also speculated by some that this is the River's namesake. Others say the river was named after a white settler by the name of Obediah.). Also, Chief Double Head had made a name for himself. As I understand, he was Nettlecarrier's brother (speculation). These names gathered as leaders in there tribes. They were strong men.

Without question, Nettlecarrier was a remarkably intelligent man. He soon became a spokesman and mediator between the Cherokee and the white men moving into this area. And he was one savvy negotiator and leader. Let me explain why.

The world knows that there was finally a "Trail of Tears", once the white man had trounced the Native Americans in the late 1840s (or there about) all across eastern America. But Nettlecarrier, our last great chief—saw the *beginning of the end.*

He saw what lie ahead for he and his tribe. There would be no way to retain their lands here in the valley. He knew he and his people would be forced to leave. He knew he had no viable chance to save grace for his people. But he had a plan to make the best of the horrendously bad situation. This crafty fellow made the rules when there weren't any rules. He pulled a fast one on those forcing him to leave. He was this nation's first *slick car salesman*...if you will. Before moving his people away, Nettlecarrier elected to *sell* his countless acres of land. No, he didn't just leave. He sold the Obey River land to the unsuspecting white settlers moving here. This is where it gets touchy.

Nettlecarrier deeded property to many of this community's early settlers. The acres of land owned by William Dale were sold to him by the Cherokee (where our dam is located). There was a middle man that handled some of the paperwork, but his land came via the Cherokee tribe and Nettlecarrier.

Edward and Sara Irons had purchased their land from the Cherokee also. Most of what is now Irons Creek was their family homestead. But there was trouble brewing.

Just as Nettlecarrier and his tribe were leaving out, our country was recovering from the Revolutionary War. Our nation was deeding lands to veteran soldiers returning from this war, and those soldiers willing to move west of the New England states were granted land as payment for their services in the fight. As these soldiers began moving to these deeded lands, they quickly found that other angry settlers had already set up homes and farms—and they held deeds of their own.

As one can imagine, the Cherokee contracts with their lack of legal wording and proper national seals were considered of little value to our country's leaders. Edward Irons actually purchased his land twice, just so he and his family could remain near the Obey River that they loved.

William Dale's contract was allowed to remain, but its acreage was drastically reduced. The original Cherokee contract stated that William owned "all of the lands drained by the Obey River". Now that's a big chunk of property. But William and his wife, Rachel Irons Dale, retained 449 acres in their own hollow down by the dam. It was, and still is, the Dale Hollow.

So Nettlecarrier and his followers made their move west. Many relocated in Oklahoma, and some as far west as Texas and Arizona. The move was just as harsh as the history books state, and many lost their lives along the way. But Nettlecarrier and a band of braves would come back to their hollows during winter in the years that followed the move. The hunting grounds here were considerably better here than in their new home. The home site of Edward Irons would be transformed into a small city of teepees and Cherokee hunters for weeks during the numerous winters that followed after their initial move. Edward and Nettlecarrier were good friends, even after their bout with the government.

And so it was that the Cherokee were forced out. They gave up and left. But thanks to the crafty efforts of Chief Nettlecarrier, the tribe left rich. And there's something to be said for that.

The following are some examples of local Native American hand tools. Of course, it is illegal to remove artifacts from Corps property, but many of the farm fields nearby have been surface hunted for arrowheads and Indian artifacts. All of these shown belong to different collectors nearby and would be considered part of the Obey River Culture. Though not from the actual river, the nearby fields offer us a glimpse into our ancient culture of long ago. Enjoy.

*Plainview Point, knife, and Handheld Scraper
Found near Wolf River*

*Hamilton Point, Gum Grove Area, Pickett County
Lauren Shell Collection*

Collection of Points from the Obey River Culture
Author's Possession

Points of the Obey River Culture, Author's Collection

Author's Collection

Necessities

Contents of an old trunk and a young heart.

Miss Margaret Fleming rode quietly in the back of a covered wagon through the rugged wilderness of the Appalachian Mountains. It was the year 1850. She was on the longest trip of her life, leaving the eastern hills of her youth and making her way westward to a new and exciting settlement in the middle Tennessee hills. She was alone in the world, having only her older sister and brother-in-law as family companions. She was joining them on this long journey, hoping for a new life and a new home. Margaret was moving to Willow Grove.

On this journey, Margaret carried only the most essential of necessities along with her. All of which were tucked snuggly into a very small trunk. She had only the clothes on her back and four items. These were the four things she held most dear in life. Two items were family bibles, with names and relations dating back to the old country. In them, she reread the names of the ones she loved, those left behind in the move. They were bittersweet treasures to her—subtle reminders of the loved ones she missed so very much. They were her strongholds in life.

Another item was the trunk itself. It held her precious belongings safe for hundreds of miles of rough and tumble land. It kept her last great possession held tightly within, and it did so her whole life.

The last item was the quilt her mother made for her in the year of her birth. In 1833, Margaret's mother hand-pieced and hand-quilted this one of a kind quilt with loving hands. It warmed her when she was cold and comforted her when she was down. It was the greatest gift of her early life.

Margaret soon found the love of her life in this new home, and she became Mrs. Margaret Fleming Stone. The branches of her family tree include the name Stone, McClusky, Dulworth, Upchurch, and many more down the line after Willow Grove.

I mention this wonderful red and white quilt for a reason. This quilt is still in existence—still resting where Margaret placed it a century and a half ago. This 180 year old family heirloom is still tucked away in that same little trunk now resting in Livingston, Tennessee. It is now with Margaret's Great, Great Granddaughter, Mrs. Christine Upchurch. A former resident of Old Willow Grove, Christine has given me tons of wonderful and historical stories dating back to her precious Willow Grove days. To me, *she* has been a great treasure. She has invited me into her home and allowed me to copy her many fantastic pictures, many of which are strewn about my books and articles. She also allowed me to hold that beautiful old quilt. I was almost frightened by its touch, fearing I'd mar this great old antique of Willow Grove.

1833 Quilt from Willow Grove

We have been unable to determine this unique pattern stitched into its surface. The bright red patches are not familiar to any quilters we've shown. In fact, Christine tells me several quilters from Old Willow Grove once tried to recreate the pattern with no success. It may very well be unique, improvised in the early nineteenth century by Ms. Margaret's loving mother.

I still visit Christine whenever I get the chance. She jokes about being old, but her youthful ninety-one year old eyes shine with the rich history she's shared with me. I owe much of my historical writings to her generosity and kindness. She's a dear friend, and a necessity of my own. ~

Ms. Christine Upchurch, 2006

Soaring with the Eagles

By: Mark Willis
Park Ranger
Dale Hollow Lake

There's certain "necessities" that visitors to Dale Hollow Lake almost always seem to bring – sunglasses, fishing gear, sunblock, and beach towels. But the essentials are a bit different for the visitors who plan to attend Dale Hollow Lake's popular Eagle Watch event.

Instead of swimsuits and sandals, the Eagle Watch participants will be wearing earmuffs, and parkas, because this Corps of Engineers sponsored event is held annually on the third and fourth Saturday in …(brrr)…January.

With binoculars and cameras draped around their necks and a thermos of hot coffee in hand, the raptor enthusiasts board an open barge at the boat ramps of Lillydale Campground and Dale Hollow State Park for a two-hour excursion on the lake. During each cruise the excited participants will get a rare opportunity to watch our national symbol soaring overhead, or perched high atop a tree overlooking beautiful Dale Hollow Lake.

Corps of Engineers' Barge and Spectators
Eagle Watch Event

Dale Hollow Lake has the second-largest wintering bald eagle population in the state of Tennessee. The ice-free waters and ample food supply of Dale Hollow Lake provide an inviting destination for these northern eagles who have been forced south by severe winters in the north, which can threaten the birds and freeze their food source.

Since its inception in 1980, this unusual event has grown in popularity, and perhaps the best measure of the success of this event is not in the actual number of visitors who participate, but in the number who return. The free interpretive outings soon became so popular that a reservation system was implemented. The tours also provided a benefit to the Corps and the surrounding communities by bringing visitors to the lake at a time of year when tourism is sparse.

The planning of an Eagle Watch is begun well in advance, and the Corps has strengthened its ties with a number of other organizations because of the inter-agency cooperation and assistance that is needed to conduct this program. The Kentucky State Trooper Island Youth Camp, a summer camp sponsored by the Kentucky State Police, provides an additional barge and staff to assist in transporting participants.

Even local community members are involved in staging the event. Some nearby residents are members of The Friends of Dale Hollow Lake, Inc., a non-profit organization of volunteers who frequently offer assistance to the U.S. Army Corps of Engineers on worthwhile environmental projects. During this program these volunteers donate and serve complimentary hot drinks and donuts for all Eagle Watch participants. These refreshments are served in one of the Dale Hollow State Park buildings just above the state park ramp.

Approximately 150 participants are on board for each tour and Corps of Engineers Park Rangers are always on hand to mingle among the crowd, answering questions or assisting visitors in using a telescope to get an even closer look at that perched or soaring eagle.

Since 1980, this event has offered hundreds of members of the public their first opportunity to observe our national symbol in its natural habitat. There are few experiences more exhilarating than spending a cool, crisp morning watching these magnificent raptors performing rarely-seen mating flights or diving at waterfowl for food.

Individuals who wish to make reservations for the Eagle Watch should call the Resource Manager's Office at (931) 243-3136 each year on or after November 15th.

If you happen to be fortunate enough to get a space on the next Eagle Watch tour, take a good look around as you're loading the barge, and you may notice there's something in the air besides the chill – it's excitement.

Crowd of Frigid People on the Eagle Watch

A Fish Tale

By Sheryl Shell

E. C. Reagan and his collection of Muskie mounts

In every small community it seems one person "stands out" from the rest. In the Willow Grove and Lillydale area of Dale Hollow Lake, that man is E.C. Reagan.

"Come and listen to a story about a man named Ed...

Edward E.C. Reagan was born in 1931 and raised in Clay Co., Tennessee by his parents, Elbert and Dolly. This family lived the river days before the lake was constructed, and E.C. still lives, loves and enjoys the lake today.

He married Jo Adele Hagan in 1951. On the day his son, Clark, was born at the Lady Ann Hospital in nearby Livingston, he was being deployed to the Korean War. That's right, folks, he never got to see that son until his return. He also has a daughter, Rita, and he is devoted to his four grandchildren and four great-grandchildren.

When times got hard, E.C. took his family to Greenwood, Indiana and did masonry work, but his thoughts always brought him back to Willow Grove. In 1968, he bought a little block store building, located about four miles up the road from Willow Grove Marina, from Willie "Snake" Colson where he sold bait, ice and gas. He would arise, on any given day, and drive clear to Glasgow, Kentucky in his old pick-up truck and haul back nine, 300# blocks of ice to sell to his loyal customers. I can't help but wonder—what did those blocks weigh when he arrived back home on those hot summer days? It didn't matter to him. He was doing what he loved and also making a living for his family.

Locals trading knives at Reagan's Grocery, about 1970

In the early 1980's, E.C. and Jo bought what once was the Fairview Methodist Church building and land just across the road, where they operated Reagan's Grocery until 1987. But even after the sale of that business and home, his roots still remained right here on Willow Grove Highway, and only a few miles up the road.

Reagan's Grocery, late 1970s

E.C. has always enjoyed fishing on Dale Hollow Lake and has taken numerous friends and acquaintances with him trolling for the yet bigger prize muskellunge. "I always trolled with a wooden, Model A Bomber #6, and I always had faith the next **big one** was just across that next point." And, sure enough, the "trophies" on his wall prove that. On the coldest, windiest, and worst day of winter, he would drop his boat in the water and return with a smile on his face. "Got a good one today, Larry," he would yell as he packed up to head home. And Larry Shell, owner of Willow Grove Marina, would nod his head thinking what determination and dedication that neat ol' fellow possessed.

As we reminisced in his photos, he pointed out one particular fish picture and said, "That one got me $100.00 ---best pay ever. Actually, only pay ever!" Now, let me tell all of you, my jaw dropped on that one as all this time I thought he was a hired guide. No wonder the avid fishermen kept returning year after year for his expertise. Cool fellow, don't ya think?

E. C.'s $100 Muskie, about 1998

He did tell me of his most frightening moment on the Dale. In the fall of 1978, he and his son-in-law were running hard up Mitchell Creek, when the steering cable broke on his 50 h.p. Johnson motor and he was thrown out and into the cold water. As consciousness returned, his main thought was with the boat and motor circling back to run over him. One scary moment, I don't care who you are! With the help of his son-in-law who remained in the boat, and the good Lord above, he is still with us today.

Now, this tale wouldn't be complete without a fish story. He has a few. He beamed with pride as he told these two. On Christmas Day, for four straight years, he had caught a trophy "Muskie". The weather was so vile on the fifth year, he bowed out. He was jinxed from thereon. His lucky cycle depleted. His other fond story was quite a tale. He latched onto a nice "wall hanger", but after the battle was done, and he pulled in his line, all he reeled into the boat was that old wooden Bomber with three Muskie teeth imbedded within. Now, you be the judge! Does this sound like a fish story to you?

E. C. Reagan and a prize walleye, 2007

Today, you may still see E.C. headed for the lake, but it won't be on those cold, blustery mornings. He chooses the warm afternoons when the walleye will gulp his Model A #9 Bomber or his Reef Runner. And, of course, as long as his health continues, he will hunt and find the occasional arrowhead on our rich grounds near the lake.

So, *"This poor ol' mountaineer kept his family fed,"* …

And he enjoyed life in the fullest while doing so. Here's hoping you have many more casts, my friend! ~

A Day on the Wolf River

With Kayak Guide Jesse Walton

On certain trips I like to tell tales of a cavern hidden beneath the hills. This cavern forms one stream of one of the Three Forks of the Wolf River. Tales of horror and hope can both come from the waters that bubble up from this chasm. The tale I find most true is the story of the World's Largest Smallmouth Bass, not the one caught in the early years of Dale Hollow… the ones that live in the chasm beneath the mountain. You see, every spring the Smallmouth bass on Dale Hollow make their spawn run up the Wolf River, they can be found in all the deep holes throughout the following summer, but sometimes, when the Wolf truly roars with the Spring rains, a few of these bass go all the way up.

For over twenty miles they swim against the flow, and sometimes over the dam itself at the Alvin C. York Gristmill. This happens very rarely for the Wolf must indeed be swollen to unthinkable heights for the bass to maneuver the dam, but it has happened. For those few that cross over there will soon be three choices; follow one of the small creeks to their ultimate doom beneath one of the mountain's many small waterfalls, turn around and go back, or follow the current of the cold spring water that flows from beneath the mountain. Local farmers tell tales of giant bass found dead in their fields, but no tales can be told of what lies beneath the mountain for none there have ventured to tell. I have stood and looked into that chasm. Clear but dark water indeed comes from beneath the mountain, both clear as crystal and cold as ice. There must be some inhabitants to this dark underground realm, but that is another story. Today, I'm going to take you kayaking down the Wolf.

It is here at the fissure that we shall begin our long journey of the Wolf River, here at its mountain base where deep mysteries begin to cloud your mind. We have driven up from Upchurch Road, the one with the big NO OUTLET sign, and now our kayaks are resting by the river just a few yards down from where the water first comes from the fissure and then goes through the natural tunnel underneath the road itself. We watch as the drop off vehicle pulls away and now, with the proper gear for a day's adventure; rope, vests, medical kit, water, food, fishing rods, camera, bilge pump, cooler and extra paddles, we begin our expedition. Within the first hour we have winded through the large valley often hugging the Northern range of mountains but eventually winding back to the Southern side. The mountainous backdrop is beautiful and the stone pebble floor over which we paddle truly shows that this stream has been here far longer than any man could tell. We are paddling through the Valley of the Three Forks of Wolf River.

There is a decent current here due to the rains over the past few days, the water is less than a foot deep in most places and the stream only a few yards wide. It is however getting larger. This mysterious stream is one of many that will eventually join just above the York Grist Mill. We are beside the road now and going under our first bridge, this means that we are just a short ways from Blowing Cave, and now we see it in the distance. Large rusted iron blocks us from entering the cave itself but as we peer between the bars, with a bit of imagination, we can see a small pile of bones towards the back of the cave; at least as far back as we can see. Perhaps your eyes are sharper than mine, can you see beyond the bones? Was that a cat that I just saw peering through the darkness? Well, I'm not really sure either, whatever it was we can both agree that it was only half there.

Mouth of Blowing Cave

Did you see the shadows moving in the deep hole before the gate? I'm going to take a few quick casts, you can join me if you'd like. BAM! In a second my pole is doubled over and a moment later the line snaps as waves disappear into the cave. Perhaps it was a Smallmouth who made the journey some years ago or maybe a trout desiring the frigid cold waters of the cave. At any rate it's gone now.

Let me tell you a tale about this cave, true or not who now lives to tell the difference? Blowing Cave is what we call it, but if you want to do your own investigating you'd have to look for the Wolf River Cave. The deep darkness into which you're looking now continues for nearly eight miles making it the seventh longest cave in Tennessee. For eight miles the darkness is complete and in ages long ago this darkness was home to the banshees of old. Perhaps it houses them still. The old tales tell of a black malice living here, with a scream as that of a tortured woman. When settlers first came to this valley, they prospered off of the rich soil in abundance around the river. Homes were built, and families began, and life seemed to be good for these early farmers. However, on the darkest nights of the year, screams of death and pain would pierce through the darkness and send fear into the hearts of the bravest men. On nights like these, there would be no sleep in the valley; when the morning came, there was never any trace of the intruder. Only missing goats or sheep—no blood, no tracks, no trail.

And so the tales were begun. Years came and went, but before long, brothers were fighting and dying in this once peaceful valley. The war had come, and here more than anywhere else the line between Blue and Grey was as thin as thread and the loss of both sides was a heavy hurt to the souls of all. But some men wore no uniform and fought with deadly malice.

The tale I tell is of such a group of men, men reputed by the North to be without mercy and by the South to be heroes without discretion. In the Cumberland Platcau, they are infamous as the Guerillas that ravaged the countryside. They share two tales along the banks of the Wolf River, the second is historically true and proven, but this, the first, may only be legend. This tale is of Champ Ferguson and the Banshees of Blowing Cave. But again, it is for another day and time, we have a river to paddle, you know!

Shortly after leaving Blowing Cave we find ourselves paddling past muddy banks and fallen trees. The clear water is beginning to change to dark brown, and after passing this next bend the current will pick up from the other streams joining ours. Oh yeah, first we've got to go under this small bridge –watch your head! Bend after bend after bend, we go, and over the course of the next hour we find ourselves in the middle of the valley. We cannot see the mountains in the distance because the overhanging trees are just starting to bloom. From where we sit, all we can see is the green and blue tunnel we're paddling through. The water is beginning to clear up some, not much but some. The banks are green grass and the water is in that grass; the river is still high. This is a good sign for us, though it could have rained for weeks before the river can change in a single day, and without high water this trip would not be possible. At the moment it means that we won't have to portage over the shoals coming up at the Rotten Fork. You'll smell the sulphur soon and understand the name. This is where our stream joins forces with Little Jack Creek to truly become the Wolf River. Until this point, we have been paddling the mysterious stream through private property, didn't say so earlier 'cause I didn't want to make you nervous. The farmers normally only shoot at me when they're growing more than tobacco, or if they hear the screams of a woman. Better lower your complaints, by the way; I'll tell you the story of the cave on some other trip; I promise.

For a moment I forget about you, my companion, and visions fill my mind and the valley in which I paddle suddenly becomes my home—the dark green hills in the distance seem to rush towards me as if I'm flying on eagle's wings. With my long hair brushing against my face in the breeze, I see that I am in fact dashing across the valley on the back of a tall painted horse as I ride off to hunt the Banshees that I know must be made of flesh and blood. Some brave farmers are with me also and by the loudening cries rising with the moon, I know that we are getting closer to the lair. We are riding towards Blowing Cave. Tonight we will find this unseen foe and vanquish it from our lands forever… Wait, that's not me. I'm in the mind of someone else, or as most folks call it, simply day dreaming.

I've forgotten to tell you the names of the creeks we've passed, not that you'd care as mesmerized as you are with the scenery. The Shoals we just passed through are caused from the junction of Little Jack Creek, which is really the combined streams of Bud Creek, Jim Creek, Stokes Creek, Rocky Creek and Falling Water

Creek. Just back a ways we've already passed Delk Creek, Little Dry Creek and Big Dry Creek. We are going to be passing plenty more and as each one finishes it's own separate journey to join with the Wolf I'd like to remind you of how far a simple creek can go. I'm going to share the Wolf with you, the Wolf that eventually flows into Dale Hollow Lake (the Obey River.) But before I share any more of this beautiful river, I find it important to tell you where it's really going. Of course the Obey River exits the Dale Hollow Dam and then joins the Cumberland River. From there the water winds its course through locks and dams all the way to the Ohio River, and then the Mississippi. From there, the Gulf of Mexico and the ocean; you see this very water that's dripping from your paddle now, even the single bead of sweat that is running down your face, will all take this journey. It's the amazing thing that so few people comprehend. That cigarette I watched you flick into the river against my direct orders not to, I wonder how many people will see it before it eventually deteriorates? The banshees of Blowing Cave, I wonder if any have ever died to float down the river to the sea, (before the locks and dams)? I just wonder, and I want to share that wonder with you. This is more than just a river; it is the pulsing vein of life for the world. This river is every river for every river is connected through the deep bonds instilled by the Master Creator at the beginning of time. Now, you know what, we are really paddling; let's continue.

If you look up ahead in the distance you can start to see the Swinging Bridge that leads to Sgt. Alvin C. York's grave. I'll share a bit of his story with you, but his son Andy will happily share more if you just ask, he's at the store just across from the gristmill, we'll be there in about half an hour. Of course I didn't know him, but the history books have him remembered as the most decorated soldier of the First World War. He ran the mill where we'll have to portage the dam in just a short time. This was his home, as a boy I can see him sitting on that rock ledge to your right with a cane pole in his hands. As a man, I can see him adjusting the gears on the mill as we pass by. As a hero, I see him as a man who fought for our freedom to paddle these waters. As a legend, I see him still, paddling his canoe right beside you, never really leaving this Valley, his home. Close your eyes and maybe you'll see him too.

Alvin C. York Grist Mill

As for the rest, you'll just have to go and ask Andy. I'm sure you've noticed that the current is all but totally gone now, we are in the deep pool before the dam. Go ahead and take some casts while we're here; there are plenty of bass and trout in these deep green waters, though they are still a bit muddy.

Glad to see you've caught some fish; wish I'd had the same luck. We're going to have to take out here, just beside the Mill. I'll go first and then pull you up. Go ahead and take some pictures while we're here and have a look around, there's a restroom just over yonder. The gristmill is an amazing sight along the Wolf River, as my companion is off exploring I decide to check the waters downstream. Today it looks as if the water is a bit shallow to make the trip, and within my range of vision I can see two logjams just ahead. Using my discretion as a guide, I decide that today may not be the best time to finish this trip. I call back the transportation and as we're waiting for a ride we decide to go ahead and have lunch at one of the many picnic tables. No, no, the trip is not over! We are just going to cut out a few miles, ok, about seven miles really. We'll leave it for another day! We are going to be dropped off at Burnt Mill Ford now. From there, we'll paddle down to Gunnel's Fishing Camp and the beginning of Dale Hollow Lake. I'll share the historical Champ Ferguson tale towards the end of the trip. Are you ready for the story to continue?

We are back on the water now, just below the bridge. A friend of mine lives in that house there and we're okay to put in here, as long as you're with me. I can't tell you about the small dam just upriver there—you see we've cut that part of the story out for today; it belongs to that stretch of river and that is another journey. The terrain is much different here—we are no longer paddling a small meandering stream, we are now deep in the heart of the Wolf River. From here, the river men once rafted their long haul down through the shoals and around every bend. There were not so many of them up this far, but they were here once. I'll have to guide you a bit more aggressively from here on. This will be a solid class II rapid for part of the trip. There will be some nice swimming or fishing holes however.

Just ahead I want you to hug the right bluff and shoot for where the water is at its whitest point. The ideal is to find the V's and cut through them without bumping any rocks that would hinder your balance. Good, you've made it through! Now, hug your left side, don't get too close to the cliff though… paddle, PADDLE NOW! Left stroke, LEFT STROKE! Good Job! Go straight through the middle of this next set! MIDDLE, not left! OK, good job. Look at that waterfall on your right; beautiful isn't it? Now eyes forward, if you get hung up, just wait for me; that's why I'm behind you, not to mention you couldn't hear me if I was up there! Just think, there's barely enough water to paddle this today—last week these waves were five foot high from all the rain! After this next bend it will calm down for a while and we'll talk some more. Hug the right now!

Water's about a foot and a half deep now, in the holes it can get past the paddle- I don't really know how deep it is. Some say there are holes twenty feet deep on the river. Some say holes like that are where the next world record bass will come from. During the summer months, this water will be less than eight inches deep in most stretches; and just last week, with all the spring rains, the water here was around ten feet deep and could have swallowed you alive. I've gone under in that mess before, with logs passing you on either side, and the waves reaching six feet tall, it's not whitewater kayaking; it's kayaking the spring floods, and this can be immensely dangerous.

Looking up into the hills on either side you should be able to see the waterfalls still pouring out a small but steady stream of rainwater. The trees aren't in full bloom yet, so this is a great time for viewing the countryside. Look, there on the far bank! Coyotes are all over this river! One or two don't pose any threat, but we don't want to paddle into the middle of a large group. After the flood waters cattle can sometimes be washed downstream from that farm we just passed, or the others upriver. I've paddled through a pack of these coyotes before, on a different river. It is a very unnerving feeling to pass between the middle of a pack of hungry animals knowing that you are interrupting their lunch.

Times like those, it's nice to have a seven-foot wooden paddle in your hands!

No, they're not going to get us; they're just part of the beautiful nature found on this river. Go ahead and start casting for a while, it'll be flatter water for a good ten minutes now. There you go! Don't let it get to those logs up ahead! Nice fish, I'd put it at about four pounds. Just keep on casting! I've gotten one now, not quite as big though. This bridge we're getting ready to go under is simply called the Ford Road Bridge. BOOM... BOOM BOOM, BOOM! They don't normally come after us this far; it was nice knowing you my friend! This is the part where my security waiver really starts to pay off! Just kidding, there is a county shooting range just ahead and it seems that some of the local officers are out practicing. We could provide them with a moving target... No? If you say so, HEY!! Paddlers coming through, cease fire guys! Beautiful day so far, just passed some coyotes up the way, no doubt scared off by ya'll. Have a good one.

The next couple of hours are spent fishing. I have to shout a few more orders over this course of river, and I can see that you're curious about Molly Lowery Road, the road going right through the river. Yes, it is a public road despite all the no trespassing signs. No, the folks in that house on the right don't have to cross the river every day; the road comes from both sides. There are going to be some really beautiful waterfalls coming up. There is one part of this trip that I would wish you couldn't see. We'll be there within the hour.

We've passed some small cascading waterfalls now, but this one is not so pretty. This is a testament to the terms "Redneck" and "Trailer Trash." This is the one spot where my temper always flares at the idiocracy and self-centeredness of man. Here the entire mountain is covered in trash, from top to bottom, straight up the bluff. We'll be seeing bits and pieces of it for the rest of the trip; all of the beautiful scenery from here on will have some sign of man in it. I don't know what kind of person can be so cheap and moronic as to not haul it off to the dump, or at least bury or burn it in their own yard. The respect for nature has faded from our world and again I remind you that this river will eventually become the lake; this trash will not deteriorate and will likely find a final resting place in some cove on Dale Hollow. Not everything in life is beautiful.

Let's just keep paddling, I really wish you didn't have to see that mess back there; I really wish some people would have better souls. I'm going to be quiet for a while, just let you enjoy it for yourself; you have two eyes and ears. I don't have to point out the tall patch of Pine on the far mountain there or quickly blooming Dogwood trees on the flat stretch of shore to our right. The turtles resting on that log just ahead of us and the wood ducks that have just spotted us coming down river; you can see all of that for yourself. I'll explain why we haven't seen any Great Blue Herons yet in just a short while. Enjoy the silence, the river is calm now and the sun's reflection on the water is slightly mesmerizing; just take it all in and let your soul be at rest. That whistling chirp is a King Fisher, look there he goes! Close your eyes for a spell and venture into the past…

King Fisher

HEAVE, HO, HEAVE, HO…
Chop those logs boys and pile em' high.
Chop those logs boys and prepare for the ride.
Gather em' up and roll em' down.
Tie em' up and anchor em' sound.
Soon the rains again will come.
Soon the waters again we'll run.
HEAVE, HO, HEAVE, HO my lads…

Farther and farther let your mind still fly,
Farther and farther till two pasts collide.

In the river what is that?
Matted fur and body all Black.
Swimming for us now boys,
Larger than the bear.
Make steady yer axes boys,
make steady yer feet.
Ignore it's cries of death and pain,
today we see the banshee plain.
No darkness now can hide its cruel cat shape,
Tis' more than legends now we face.
Steady boys, swing with force.
Steady boys, we shall change its course.
See how it limps, see it's blood?
Surely war with it twas raised.

The farmers that rode had met this foe
The farmers that rode shall ride no more.
Only one with a tale to tell,
Only one that escaped from Hell

Now it comes yet again,
Nearer and nearer the mighty River Men
Now it comes in full light of the morn'
Nearer and nearer to it's bloody end.

Tales would be told of the fight that day
Legends made of men's renown
Brave men sent to an early grave
Though many lived others did die
And though the beast was thought killed,
It's body again was lost in the tide.

Deep in the Obey the horror now lies
Dark depths of the lake silence it's cries
Darkness again it now calls home
Deep in the caves of the Obey
Banshees still roam…

Back Bone Bridge

Wake up! PILLARS AHEAD! We're going under the Back Bone Bridge now (295.) Just don't hit the pillars and you'll be ok. Be sure to wave at the Cook family up on the banks there; a wonderful family with the best view of the river I've found to date. This is one of the prettiest falls we've seen yet; of course you can see it for yourself though; can't you? Whistle a tune for me if you don't mind, legend tells that the whistling can summon thunder on the river. You don't believe me? Keep whistling! Thud, thud, thud THUD, THUD, THUD; can you feel the rumble? Can you see the ripples dancing across the water? Don't look so amazed; it's not magic… or even legend! Look to the left, it's a small herd of horses and mules. They like to follow along till the end of the fence line.

Now we're coming up on the only island, no official name but I call it Turkey Island. We'll be going to the left today, against the cliff. Not enough water on the right branch. Look ahead in the trees and you'll understand the name a bit better, they're almost always here. Of course there's also a beaver dam just ahead, though I'm sure it's been washed away by last weeks rain. Yep, no signs left of a years work for Mr. Beaver. This had been a good deep hole for the Red Eye last summer. After a few more bends in the river you see your first Blue Heron of the day. Keep your eyes open; you're getting ready to see lots more. They nest here every year and today you'll be able to see the young hatchlings peering out over the feeble stick nests. Circling above us now I count eleven total adults and two more still in the trees; what's your count? These guys are normally very solitary; they sure don't like to share sections of the river. This is the season of love however, in the spring they work together as a colony; here there's close to a dozen nests. On the Cumberland River I've encountered colonies nearly three times as large. Just more of nature's beauty.

Hey look up ahead; a couple of river otters sliding down by Lick Creek. That means there's probably some bass up there, better take a few more casts. Can't ever catch too many can you? You know we've had fish to pull us back up river before… looks like you're experiencing that now! Is it fighting a lot or just pulling? Sounds like you've hooked into a big ole river cat, just keep wearing him out! Thirty minutes later and back by the island you're hefting seventeen pounds of river cat into your boat. If you don't mind we'll go ahead and keep this one for supper! We'd better go ahead and bucket some Smallies two if we're going to grill em' up tonight.

One last set of rapids up here and then we're going to be on flat water. Good job, you've handled all the rapids well and you've listened to me well enough to stay dry! From here on it'll be flat water, really flat water. This is all backed up from the lake, we're still about three miles from Gunnel's Fishing Camp but there will be no current this time of the year. This next bend is going to put us at the Highway 111 Bridge. Just after that bridge is a public boat ramp and a small creek joining the Wolf. The concrete foundations on either side of us are from the first bridge long ago. This is my last tale for today, one that I promised hours ago. It was here that Champ Ferguson had his historical visit to the Wolf River.

Hale's Mill used to sit beside that creek on our right, probably about where that boat ramp is now. Jonathan D. Hale was a Union man who had moved here from New Hampshire and though the Mill appeared to be prospering, fate would not permit it to survive for long. John Zachary hid in the bluffs overlooking the mill, the same bluffs that we just passed, and from that hiding place shot and killed Lafayette Allen, a Confederate soldier. Shortly afterward, Ferguson's Guerillas burned the mill to the ground. Jonathan Hale and his family safely escaped and later testified at the trial of Champ Ferguson in Nashville.

My house sits on top of the mountain we passed twenty minutes ago, just a mile up the road from where Hale's Mill once stood. In the valley beneath my home there runs the creek that we just passed. In that valley the creek flows over a large waterfall, at the base of this waterfall there is a large stonewall; it looks to me as if it were a well-protected camp at one time. I have heard no historical tales or claims to the origin of this wall; it is clearly man made and also turns this small box canyon into a very impenetrable campsite. The truth is that the Wolf River was a major location for the Civil War, not all tales of valor or deception have survived to be told today. Perhaps the history of what I call the Waterfall Wall is such a tale. Perhaps I'll share my rendition of it on another journey.

Highway 111 Bridge (previously Hwy 42)

By now we are coming to an end of our day—that's Gunnel's Fishing Camp up in the distance and for now we must leave the Wolf to go on with our ever so busy lives. I thank you for paddling with me today, and I hope that some of the wonder of the past and the beauty of the present has rubbed off on you. I'll have your fish cleaned and fried back at the shop, so be sure to stop back in, and don't forget to leave your tip!

Gunnel's Fishing Camp, Dale Hollow Lake

The Settlers, the Soldiers, the Guerillas, the River Men, and the Indians... all at some time called Wolf River their home. The Banshees and the ghosts still do... If ever you venture to the iron gates of Blowing (a.k.a. Bunkum) Cave in the dark, listen close for the cry and look deep into the blackness beyond the gates... the fierce yellow cat's eyes are watching! If you don't believe my tale, at least the small bits you've heard so far, maybe you should ask yourself one question... Why did they REALLY put those gates there?

There are still many tales that I've left untold about the Wolf River, none the least of these is the origin of the river's name. I suppose that you'll go paddling with me again though, so I had better save some tales for the next journey into the Valley of the Three Forks of Wolf River. Beware the Banshees scream and never peer too deeply into the waters of Dale Hollow Lake. ~

~ Independence Day ~

By Sheryl Shell

Firework Barge Prior to Blast-off!

Over the years, the July 4th week-end arrives on the Dale, and the lake is always abuzz. Are there fireworks? What day? What time? Well, folks, here are the answers to those questions.

There is a very dedicated employee that works and has worked most of his adult life at Willow Grove Marina. As the years trickle by, his enthusiasm to serve the public has escalated!

What started out as a few fireworks on Independence Day, has now exploded into a "Dale Hollow National Holiday." Local police, firemen, and medical personnel cover the grounds of Willow Grove, while the Tennessee Wildlife Resources Agency and the Corp of Engineers patrol the water, all promoting safety for everyone.

The notes of *"Oh, Mickey, you're so fine...Hey, Mickey...Hey, Mickey"* fill the Colson Creek air, and local DJ and Willow Grove friend, Greg McDonald of Livingston, Tennessee, pumps out tropical summer songs and offers his personal fun atmosphere of karaoke music. It's a thumpin' good time.

Each year, when the lights go down, you can hear the voice of Marla (Shell) Beason drifting across the water and into the hollows as she sings our National Anthem.

It's always a pleasant afternoon and evening for everyone as Mickey Ledbetter, himself, ignites an awesome display of fireworks while the harbor is packed full of boats, and the shores of Willow Grove fill with spectators. It's been a yearly tradition over a decade, and if Mickey Ledbetter has anything to say about it, the tradition will continue as long as the energy and spirit of our Nation's boaters still flock to Dale Hollow.

Oh, yes, I nearly forgot…if you get to this celebration of our great nation, be sure to tell Darren and his crew how much you enjoyed the fun. They may get to see the "finale" as the pizza orders "just never seem to end." *"Just a bunch of shift work"* there, as Darren also pulls the *"Eleven to Seven."*

Lord Willing…

July 4th, no matter what day it falls on, July 4th.

At dark, no matter what time you're on, at dark.

Have a happy and safe 4th on Dale Hollow Lake.~

Spectators and Boaters Fill the Harbor
Photos Courtesy of Beth Shell

A View from Pilot Island

On the edge of the Tennessee/Kentucky State line, in the heart of the Wolf River portion of Dale Hollow rests a pleasant little island. Pilot Island stretches nearly north and south out in front of Eagle Cove Marina. Today, my old boat is pushed against the bank and tied securely to cedar stumps on the western shore. Being in the mood for a hike, I thought I'd slip up to the top of Pilot Island and take in the views. There aren't too many boats churning up the waters today, but beneath the waves there's all sorts of action. Let's hike up and look around.

The dead center of Pilot Island is its highest point. And even though it's a tough climb with a lot of brush and fallen trees, I still make it a point to stop by this little knob in Vann's Branch. Vann's Branch was the name used many years ago to describe this little community. In fact, Eagle Cove Marina was once named that also in loving respect of this quaint community of long ago.

Whew. I've made it to the top and I stand in a thicket of fallen pines. The brush is just as bad as I remember, but I can still make my way through the trees. I like it here, like many folks from old Vann's Branch.

For instance, where I stand on this high knob, was once the Phillips Cemetery. Eight known Phillips and eight unknown graves were moved from here in 1942. Eight large holes still adorn the ground at my feet. A lone foot-stone is still grown into the base of a tree, reflecting the grave of a child. It must have been a special place, and with our knowledge of *moved* graves on the lake, it still might be.

Phillips Cemetery about 1940

Let's look farther. I think I'll make my way back down off the hill and meander out to the northern point. From here, we can glance at the main lake.

To our immediate left, just beneath the surface of the water, lies a foundation just out of view. Even in low water, the stones of this old building are too deep to see from shore, but still lurk in the shaley depths of this point. They are the remnants of the Vann's Branch Meeting House, also known as the Vann's Branch Church, and also sometimes known as the Vann's Springs Church.

That's a lot of names. In all likelihood, the old church did have a good spring to feed water to its practitioners. Many buildings of its day were known as the spring that fed them.

Vann's Springs Church was most probably the local source for refreshment in the form of water and spirituality. It was a rich place indeed, regardless of your need.

Vann's Branch Meeting House, about 1940

Can't you just see little kids scampering through the yard of this local meeting house? I swear I can nearly hear those tiny voices laughing and playing while family members converse about this and that. The main road ran right across this point, so you know the world stopped by for a visit on a regular basis. The road stretching toward Lillydale finds the Sulphur School just a few hundreds yards beyond our little church here. I hear kids there too—a school bell ringing in the Obey River breeze.

This same road connects us to Lillydale a few miles downstream, and to Miller's Mill, just a couple of miles upstream. The old road takes us elsewhere, too—across the river. Straight out in front of us there was a shallow ford in the river known as the Bryson Ford. It connected our Vann's Branch families to the hollows across the river via the old road. But over there—things were just different.

Let me explain. I tend to paint a pretty picture of all the things on Dale Hollow. It's just my nature. I love it here. But at times, even here on the Dale, some folks just didn't get along. This was one of those places and times.

Long before Vann's Branch metropolised into the ten or fifteen houses it possessed when the lake came, this community had some family matters across the river. Without going into great detail, that "yonder" bunch over there had begun a bit of a feud with its south-of-the-river kinfolk. In fact, it had gotten quite out of hand, and for years the southern settlers of this stretch of river held those northern kin in ill will. *Illwill*.

Yep. Illwill Creek took its name from an old *Hatfield and McCoy* type of feud. Most of the descendents of those families today still separate that name in their speech—pronouncing it Ill-Will. And life marches on.

Not all the northerly stories from here are ill. Just a few short years ago, the Huffacre Creek cove was home to a special resident. Although many people disbelieved it, the little hollow was home to a small Cayman Alligator. No one knew for certain how he arrived here in his placid little cove, but he was definitely here, and he seemed to love it. Countless photographs floated around the marinas and campgrounds about our special friend in that hollow. But unfortunately, a couple of local fellows from nearby Albany, Kentucky, managed to capture him and relocate him to a safer environment. I kinda liked having him here on the Dale, really. He wasn't aggressive at all—and besides, I don't swim in that hollow anyway.

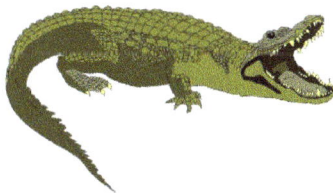

In the distance, the Kentucky State Police are shuttling passengers to and from Trooper Island from the State Park Marina on their big barge/ferry. It's a constant flow over the waves from one side to the next and back again. Just beneath those waves was the community known as Phillips Bend. Phillips and Upchurches settled in this wide and final bend of Wolf River. The long power lines overhead act as a finish line for the old river, and a State Line for us boaters—thus mingling past and present before us.

Upchurch Farm, Phillips Bend of Lillydale, early 1900s

Let's reel in our view back to our point. I've got one more story to tell about this place you'll enjoy. Take a gaze to our right. Across the lake (and the Bryson Ford of the river), we see a huge bluff overlooking the lake. That large outcropping overlook is now a housing development called Skull Bluff. It is known by that creepy name because that's what it has always been called. And it was called that for a reason.

Long before the lake was built, a man by the name of Tom Mullins owned this bluff and this stretch of river. He was a brother to a gal I often mention in my Lillydale stories by the name of Susan Mullins Biggerstaff, or "Aunt Sus". Strange as it may sound, old Tom was often referred to as Uncle Tom also. So when I mention closely-knit communities in these parts, this illustrates that point to perfection. Everybody was somebody's aunt or uncle.

But Uncle Tom had a problem. He owned this bluff and a strong sense of compassion for it. He knew that this bluff was special, and he tried to keep it secret as long as possible. Skull

Bluff was a burial ground for Native American Indians. A cave in the bluff wall housed dozens and dozens of dead bodies and the rich early American artifacts they treasured. Bags of arrowheads and clay pots filled with special river stones and fresh water pearls sat alongside these ancient rotting corpses. Lavish woven blankets covered the dead. This precious treasure trove of Native American history was a museum in and of itself. And Tom was intent on keeping it safe.

But this was Ill-Will country, and somehow word got out. A man by the name of Luke Smith began slowly and secretly raiding the cave. Before Tom knew what was happening, Luke had pilfered the vast majority of the artifacts from the site and squandered them. Tom was furious. The two had words and nearly came to blows over the deal—and their feud lasted until their dying days. Their deaths may have ended much of the ill will in Illwill.

And there you have it—the view from Pilot Island. Whether you are a grave searcher or lake lover, this place has a rich history for us all, right here on this point. And there's nothing ill about that. ~

Camp Bravehearts on Trooper Island

By: Lori Walton, Lake Times News (2007)

TFC Sutton and his staff at Trooper Island hosted Camp Bravehearts last week. Camp Bravehearts is a place where children ages 8 - 16 with congenital heart disease can enjoy summer at its best! Here it is, 10 years after the dream became reality. Camp Bravehearts celebrated their anniversary last week with the release of a beautiful hot air balloon. The campers were given the opportunity to ride the balloon, what a view it must have been! When I went for an interview with co-founder Joyce McClain, I met her with many other staff members preparing their grand celebration - 70's style. They were quite the site! She was so excited to share how this dream had become a reality. Lake Times News was honored to be a part of this celebration. Joyce had been interviewed almost a decade ago by Lake Times News, and so it was fitting for us to join the Bravehearts again. Then, and now, the staff and volunteers continue to give of themselves, to make this camp a unique and wonderful experience for children with congenital heart disease. Some of these children might otherwise never know the feeling of the outdoors as they experience it here on Dale Hollow Lake. I have always thought this was heaven on earth!

Kosair Hospital of Louisville along with CardioCare, a non-profit organization, sponsor Camp Bravehearts. The camp is staffed by volunteer doctors, nurses, parents, grandparents, and teen leaders. Many of the young campers from a decade ago carry on their involvement as teen leaders, or counselors today. This camp has meant a great deal to them! Their past experiences had such an impact that they return to pay it forward, to give back to others. This is an amazing group of people - staff and campers alike! Even grandparents working in the craft hall can be proud of their selfless involvement in this wonderful program. Genuine caring and pure hearts is what Camp Bravehearts is all about. Dr. McClain, Joyce, his wife, Dr. Boone, and all the other staff, volunteers and folks at Trooper Island deserve congratulations on a job well done!

Camp Bravehearts then - 1997, and now - 2007

CONGRATULATIONS ON 10 YEARS OF MAKING DREAMS COME TRUE!!

So, What is Trooper Island Anyway?

For years our family has buzzed by the island on one side, or slowly tooled by on the other. We always ask - what is Trooper Island? I've seen the canoes and the swimming pool from our lakeview, and the dock, with its specialty barges, but until now I had never really known their purpose.

Now that I do, I am amazed, saddened, and even encouraged to take action. Having learned their purpose awakens a feeling of responsibility. A responsibility for those less privileged - for those special kids, who for some reason or another, are not able to buzz past the island like the rest of us do. So many of us, myself included, take 'our' lake and our luxuries for granted. At Trooper Island, they give back, one child at a time. The impact results in changed lives, young people who in turn become adults who understand what giving truly means, and how far that impact reaches!

Trooper First Class Craig Sutton, Camp Director and Island Commander, met us at the dock. He was gracious and inviting, but a bit cautious too. They are well aware of all visitors to the island, it can be a bit intimidating. Realizing our purpose, he proceeded to give us a first class tour of Trooper Island. He explained its true purpose and its inner workings. Trooper Island began in 1965 as a Boys Camp. It was founded by the Kentucky State Police as a camp for under-privileged children, who would never have another opportunity to attend such a camp. Upwards of sixty kids, ages 10-12 attend their eight regular camp sessions each time throughout the summer. Then the island welcomes specialty camps, various training camps, and even honors requests by churches and other organizations. It is indeed maintained and run like a well- oiled machine. TFC Sutton takes pride in Trooper Island, and the challenges that they face. The island sits on 35 acres obviously surrounded by beautiful Dale Hollow Lake - what more could a person ask for?! The island houses its own medical center, dining hall, craft area, rec. room, and maintenance facility. There are two cabins for the boys, and two for the girls - the camp became coed about 7 years ago. There is a lodge for counselors and staff, and of course, bath houses. There is also a small nature center, and the campers themselves help to publish a newsletter. A beautiful chapel sits at the crest of the hill on the north end, overlooking the lake. Local churches donate Bibles to be available for distribution to the campers.

Each morning campers are awakened by TFC Sutton, as he drives around with his police siren blaring. The campers are offered many different types of recreational opportunities. There is a swimming pool, a shooting range, an archery range, softball diamond, and volleyball. They have a nice playground, they even had a water slide while we were there. They can go surf biking, canoeing, and inner tubing. They can fish one of the greatest lakes too! They also have a nice rec. room for those rainy days, which was made possible through several donations. We got a great tour of the weekly crafts by grandparents. Much to do makes for happy campers!

Did you know that there is a jet on Trooper Island? There are even a set of railroad tracks too!

It was incredible to visit, the island is beautifully maintained by the staff. Access to Trooper Island is by boat, everything they need must be hauled - in and out - it is a unique way to live, but they have adapted very well. As you approach the island, from the dock, the first thing that you see is a touching memorial. It is a blue light, the light is in remembrance of 24 troopers who died in the line of duty. It shines 24/7, 365 days a year. There is a beautiful resting area overlooking the lake, try to notice the light the next time you buzz by the island, and remember what it stands for. "Blessed are the Peacemakers."

The Kentucky State Police do not fund Trooper Island, it must fund itself through donations and various fund-raising activities. It costs upwards of $300,000 a year to operate and maintain Trooper Island. It is an average of $300 per child, per week of camp. If you would like to donate, or sponsor a child, all contributions are tax deductible! I know that I take it for granted that my family, my children, are able to be out on the water at Dale Hollow Lake, that we can enjoy EVERYTHING Dale Hollow has to offer. Trooper Island makes it possible for many young children to experience what many of us love, and take for granted. If you would like to take the opportunity to share your blessings, call 270-433-5422, or send a contribution.

Trooper Island is all about giving back, changing one life at a time. Thank you TFC Craig Sutton for the wonderful tour, and a big thank you to you and all your staff for the impact you continually make on young lives! God Bless!

Contributions can be sent to:
Kentucky State Police
Trooper Island Camp, Inc.
P.O. Box 473
Albany, KY 42602

Ferry Stories

In the fast paced hustle and bustle of our busy interstates, it's hard to imagine a time when speed was just not of the essence. Years ago, travelers of our roads and highways encountered many obstacles standing in the way of their roadway progress. For instance, during spring rains swollen creeks became ford of a small river, making travel difficult if not possible.

In still other places, modern bridges were built to handle the heavy traffic of a few dozen cars a day. These new-fangled and fancy iron structures were usually only one lane, forcing oncoming cars to wait until the first vehicle passed and again left the bridge open for travel.

Wolf River Bridge, about 1920

But perhaps the most interesting and unique mode of river crossing was called a ferry. Although there are still a few of these antiquated structures functioning to this day, ferries in rural areas have almost become a thing of the past.

Ferries around the Dale Hollow area, by most measurable means, were a small floating barge capable of hauling one or two vehicles over the water to the far shore. Usually there were cables fastened to each shore that the barge was fasten to, allowing it be pulled through the currents safely and quickly to its destiny.

Of course, some of these early models varied in their building much like the men who built them. Some were vast and heavy steel structures with heavy cable systems for navigation, while others were little more than wooden boxes tied with gangly hemp rope.

Obey River Ferry near Sunset Marina, 1920

*Obey River Ferry during the building
of the steel span bridge over the lake.*

There have been several sites where ferries were operated within our Dale Hollow area. The earliest was the Obey River Ferry located where the Byrdstown water plant is now. It was here long before the lake and only operated a few years until a bridge was constructed. Abutments from that first bridge still lie beneath the lake surface.

Another ferry location was the East Port Ferry which crossed the West Fork of the Obey at the East Port Marina location. It was maintained many years after the building of the lake.

Yet another ferry was the Eagle Creek Ferry, also known as the Midway Ferry that crossed Eagle Creek. Locally known as Keisling Bottom, this location still has a bridge beneath the surface near where the ferry crossed. A gravel road and launch ramp is still maintained in this location. Although many other folks were in charge of it over the years, Billy Sells and Clyde Taylor operated this ferry through the 1960s and shut it down in the very early 1970s.

Eagle Creek Ferry location at Keisling Bottom, spring, 2008

The old wooden ferry building that stood along the road is still in existence. It's been hauled up the road and now houses chickens rather than ferrymen. It's still in the care of the Sells family, just like so many years ago.

There is yet one other ferry that has operated on the Dale. In fact, it still does. It seems unlikely that such a high maintenance item could be in use in a time when machinery of all sorts make our lives easier. But there is one here. It is the Trooper Island Ferry Barge. Day in and day out the Kentucky State Police operate a shuttle between Trooper Island and the State Park Marina. It's a labor of love that keeps the Trooper Island Camp as remote and beautiful as it is. That one motorized barge is the only way to and from the island. No road connects this special place to the outside world. It is what it has always been— a separate island entity, in and of itself.

For more information on Trooper Island Boys Camp, see previous article.

Some days I take a long drive down to Keisling Bottom or maybe even out to the old East Port Ferry site. I reflect on a time I never knew, where cars sat patiently waiting on the river ferry to cart them to the far shore. These days, this antiquated old mode of travel would be a nuisance, but maybe, just maybe, it would be worth the wait. Maybe we could slow ourselves down a bit and take a look around. Maybe we could chat with the ferrymen who make their livings on the slow road, the Road Not Taken. For in a ferry world—the rush of life doesn't get in the way.

On this day, I've taken the road less traveled, *and that has made all the difference!* ~

The First Car in Old Willow Grove

Back in the days when old Willow Grove was still the thriving metropolis of eastern Clay County, Tennessee, Dr. Walter Sidwell practiced his medicine on horseback, making house calls on the many patients on his route.

Dr. Walter F. Sidwell, early 1900s

Back then, the doctors had no offices, and traveling from patient to patient was virtually the only way it was done. So, Dr. Walt Sidwell found himself a high-mileage sort of fellow.

During the 1930s, Doc had given a good bit of his care to an elderly fellow along his route. After numerous trips to this household, the old farmer simply could not pay Doc for his many hours of medical treatment. As was common in those days, the doctors of the time would often receive payment in the form of trade. Chickens and horses and even items of food would be bartered as payment. On this occasion, Doc Sidwell received a 1929 Ford Roadster.

The town of Willow Grove was all astir. Few cars were seen in the streets of Willow Grove, and certainly no one actually owned one of these new fangled machines. It was quite an eye catcher as it rumbled and rolled through town.

Doc used that same car for a few years as his chief mode of transportation, but the machine quickly wore out and found itself parked in old Willow Grove as an oddity.

When the lake came along in 1942, the car was hauled to Livingston, Tennessee, where it was again parked along the road and sat idle. A number of people inquired about the machine as it sat in its weeded confinement in town. Mr. Roy Pennington commissioned to buy the old hunk of steel and rubber, but never actually made the purchase. Randall Dulworth finally bought the old rust bucket and towed it to his family home nearby, paying a whopping $15 for his purchase.

Randall, being an ex-resident of Willow Grove, immediately recognized the machine as the one belonging to his doctor from his old home town. Randall just had to have that car.

Over the years, Randall placed a number of different engines in the car and made countless cosmetic changes on all sections of it. It made numerous trips to the races in Indianapolis, and had more used parts that original by far. In a 1992 issue of Current Lines, Carl French Ledbetter wrote an article about Randall's locally famous auto. One of the photos of the article had this inscription beneath:

"With Mileage equal to ten trips around the world on used parts, this car may hold a world record for durability."

Randall's 1929 Ford Roadster at the
Willow Grove Reunion, late 1980s
Pictured is Randall, friend, and sister, Christine Upchurch

From the streets of old Willow Grove, to the town of Livingston, this car has remained a local fixture since its humble beginning. It's hauled medications for the sick and wounded and hauled friends and family to car shows and races all over America.

Although Randall is no longer with us, his old car is still resting in his garage. And with any luck, the next generation will keep it rolling for years and years to come. ~

Atop the Water

Since the early 1950s and before, people from all walks of life have flocked to Dale Hollow for its beauty and crystal-clear water. Fishermen have called it paradise since the day our dam first began to hold back water, and have constantly studied the habitats of the fish they seek, always trying to improve their chances of netting the "big one". But another group of people have also called this utopia of contained Obey River water home for decades, too. Those are the water-skiers. And they have been here since the early days too, bringing their own brand of fun to our Dale Hollow shores. Here are some photos from over the years of our lake-loving skiers and tubers. Enjoy.

Ski Jump at Obey River Bridge, 1960s
McCormick and Winningham Crew of Livingston, TN

Dale Hollow's First Air-Chair, 1980s

*Local Boater, Jim Evans, after a successful ski run
through the Willow Grove Ski Course, 1985*

243

Jim Evans, Willow Grove Ski Course, 1985

Darren and Marla Shell Barefoot Skiing, 1986

Winners, Willow Grove Ski Course Competition
Labor Day Weekend, 1983

Local idiot, Darren Shell, Skiing on His Boat Paddle! 1986

Willow Grove Kids, 2007
Lauren, Blake, Shaela, and Paige

Darren Oliver of Livingston, TN, Wake-surfing 2007
Look, Ma...no rope!

Lauren Shell on her Sea Doo, 2007

Diary of a Bare-footer

I asked my buddy, Tom Weir, to give me a bit of history about his life for my history book. In my youth, Tom taught me the many facets of bare-foot water skiing here in our clear waters. I had learned to bare-foot a few years prior to meeting Tom, but I never had the mechanics to become a step above the common skier. Once I contacted Tom, he graciously picked me up at my marina (I was then only 14 or 15 years old), and he taught me in minutes what I had tried weeks to learn. We skied several days together here on the Dale, and I have truly enjoyed learning from this natural teacher. His ski school here on Dale Hollow was a resounding asset to the lake in those days, and Tom's techniques and friendship have stuck with a bunch of folks across the nation. I am sure many have enjoyed his friendship just like me, so I was truly humbled to receive some of his early ski pictures to grace my book. But when he wrote this little article for me, I was amazed at just how big an impact my friend, Tom, has had on the skiing world. He is a remarkable piece of Dale Hollow history. I hope you enjoy his story as much as I, for after all—I've watched him walk on water. ~

From Tom Weir, 2008

I am the fourth of 5 children of Calvin and Betty Weir, Born February 25, 1960 in a blizzard in Indianapolis, Indiana. Unable to make it to the hospital, I was born at a Sinclair gas station and was wrapped in a mechanics cloth. My other siblings are Aneta, Ginny, George, and Rob who was born in 1967. In 1963, my family started vacationing at Dale Hollow Lake and would spend between 4 to 6 weeks camping on the Island at Pleasant Grove Park on the tip of the Island. There were very few trees on the island at that time, and the ones there had very little shade. During the summer, the island was like a small neighborhood full of people camping out.

Both of my parents were skiers, and that was the family past time in the summer. I remember my mother, Betty, trick skiing at a early age. She would never get her hair wet and do 25 turns on trick skis until she would gracefully float down into the water and wave her hands signaling she was done.

I learned to ski at the age of 7, which was old in my family since the rest learned by the age of 5. I was the baby during those years and spent most of the time watching my other siblings ski. Dad "Calvin" had a rule that after 25 falls you had to take a break. It was an all day affair skiing from dusk to dawn. We have a lot of home movies of the early years, but few pictures.

In 1969, I saw my first person barefoot ski. We and about 15 other boats traveled up the lake to find calmer water to watch a guy we called Bink barefoot ski. He stepped of the ski and barefooted for about 100 yards until he fell spectacularly with several summersaults. We were all in awe. During the week that Bink camped on the island, he taught my Brother George (11 years old) to step off a ski and barefoot. George was a natural and was quickly bare-footing for several minutes across Dale Hollow Lake. After that week we never saw Bink again, but the memories of him will be with me forever.

In 1976, George finally talked me into learning how to barefoot ski. I stepped off a ski at the swinging bridge and barefoot skied deep into Indian Creek Cove. I was hooked after that moment and spent must of my summer days barefoot skiing when possible.

After graduation, I met a guy at the lake who knew how to deep water start. Incredible bare-footing without having to pick up the ski. He had learned the trick from some skiers at Cypress Gardens and taught it to me. I really had the bug then and decided to move to Winter Haven, Florida, water skiing capital of the world and home of Cypress Gardens. Once I arrived, I was in awe and just drove around and watched people ski. I quickly became friends with some of the skiers at Cypress Gardens and started learning the craft of many different types of skiing. But after a year, I decided to return to Tennessee and pursue a mechanical engineering degree from Tennessee Technological University.

Once returning in 1979, I started Weir's Ski School Celina and stared teaching others how to barefoot ski. My slogan was *learn to barefoot ski or the lesson was for free.*

I entered my first barefoot tournament in 1979 at Cypress Gardens and got second place. In 1980, I entered several other tournaments and qualified for the nationals but was disqualified from competing because I unknowingly skied in the wrong regionals.

In 1981, I was sure to pay more closely attention to the rules and won the Men's overall time in the nationals. The pictures you have of me with the "superfooter" signs were from that tournament. I also continued to teach skiing on the lake and started teaching a college course from TTU on skiing and continued teaching until 1985.

In 1982, I competed in the Masters at Cypress Gardens which was an invitational tournament for the top ten barefoot skiers in the country and got 1st in tricks. It was shown on ESPN.

In 1983, I was 1st in jumping and got 6th overall in the nationals. I had the longest jumps in the world for the years 1983, 1984.

During my years teaching on Dale Hollow Lake, I taught well over 1000 people how to barefoot ski and coached 5 other people to national championships in the divisions.

I got married in 1984 and like a lot of people started putting behind me my athletic days and pursuing other interests. After graduating from TTU in 1986 with a Bachelor of Science in Mechanical Engineering, I decided my skiing career had run its course. I moved on, pursuing other great adventures which life had to offer.

During those years, I got divorced and remarried and currently have 4 children. My wife, Vonda, had one child when we got together. Megan (16) has been a model child and I love her dearly. Our other children are Morgan (7), Maggie (5), Matthew (15 months). We currently live next to my mother, about ¼ mile above Cedar Hill Resort.

This winter I bought a new ski boat and am excited about starting a new chapter in my life on Dale Hollow with my family. This is the first time in my life that I have reflected about my experiences with Dale Hollow and skiing and can only say it was an enjoyable experience, and all has ended well thus far. It's been a great run.

Tom Weir, 1980s. Looks like fun, huh?

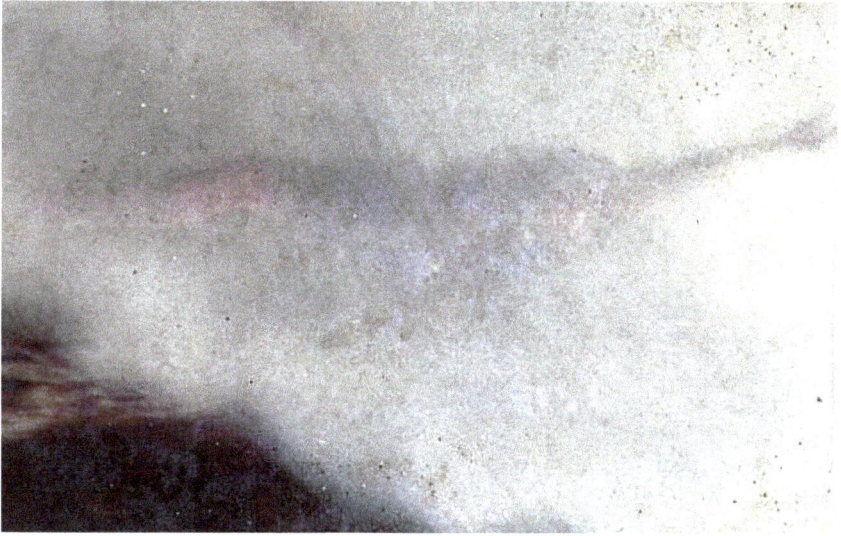

Tom Weir during Deep-water Backward Toe-hold Start

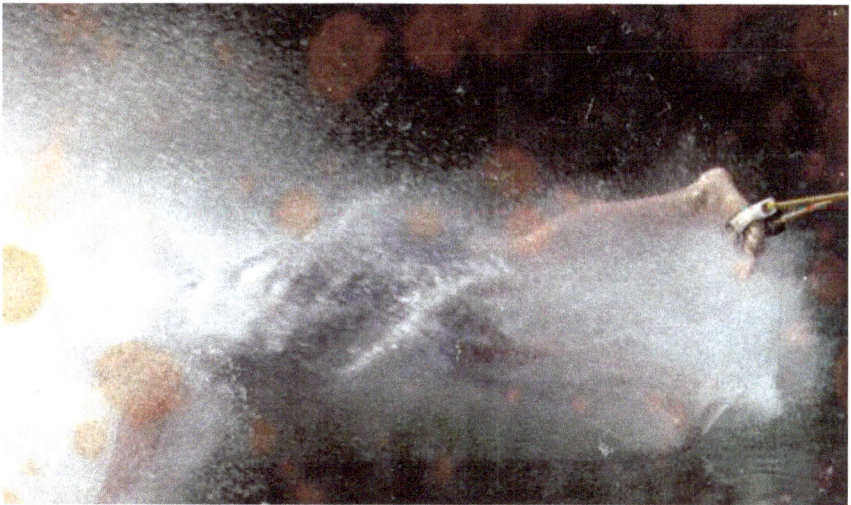

Tom Weir...nearly up!

Tom Weir, almost Standing on One Foot, Toe-hold

Tom Weir, One Foot Backward Toe-hold Deep-water Start

Tom Weir, Forward Toe-hold, One Foot

Thumbs-Up Tom!

Tom Weir and Family, 2007

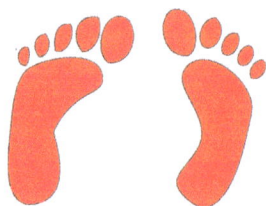

The Duck Hunters

There is yet another bunch of crazy people traversing our shores like the skiers. From the warm and balmy opening days of Teal season, to the frigid days of late December, the duck hunters of Dale Hollow have loved our waters just like the rest of us. Here are a few nice photos. Enjoy.

Cates Family, winter 2005
Wilson, Connie, and Dr. Jamie Cates
Allons, Tennessee

Connie and Dr. Jamie Cates, 1970s

Cates Crew, Teal Season, 1983

Breaking the Ice, Dr. Jamie Cates, Colson Creek, 1977

Hardy Hunter, Bill Speck of Livingston, 1978

Bill Speck at Kemper Flat (Clark Bottom), 1986

Bill Speck with Katie and Her First Duck, 2004
Speck Pictures Courtesy of Matilda Speck

Photo Gallery

Airplane lands at Willow Grove Marina, 1952

DALE HOLLOW RESERVOIR
Scene of the 1948 National Outboard Motor Races
Nashville District   Corps of Engineers

Boat Races at Cedar Hill   1948

LILY DALE SAW MILL, MERCER GROUP

Shown from left to right are, Andy Mercer, Mr. Copeland (Blacksmith), Alex Mercer, Randsom Mercer, Car- ter Mercer (Hattie Mercer his wife), Ann Mercer wife of Alex Mercer, Marth Mercer wife of Sam in the sha- dows, Mary Mercer wife of Randsom Mercer, Vena Mercer wife of Andy Mercer and Nancy, Irene, Mary, Hil- ery, Sussie, Samuel (Buddy), Johny, Sarah and Lizzle in mothers arms. All mercer children. Submitted by Sam Mercer, Lewisville, Ind. 47352

Bob and Elise Hill, Obey River Bridge 1940s?

Willow Grove Gymnasium, late 1930s

Mill Creek Falls, Sulphur Creek, Summer, 2006
Photo Courtesy of Beth Shell

Mitchell Creek 1950
Fox Springs site

First Wolf River Bridge, Early 1900s

Building the First Wolf River Bridge, Early 1900s

Second Wolf River Bridge, 1940s?

Third Wolf River Bridge after its completion and as it stands today.

Sunset Over Clark Bottom From Randall's Point of Kemper Flats

Eagle Creek Mill, near the head of Eagle Creek

Hatcher Hall Church near Eagle Creek

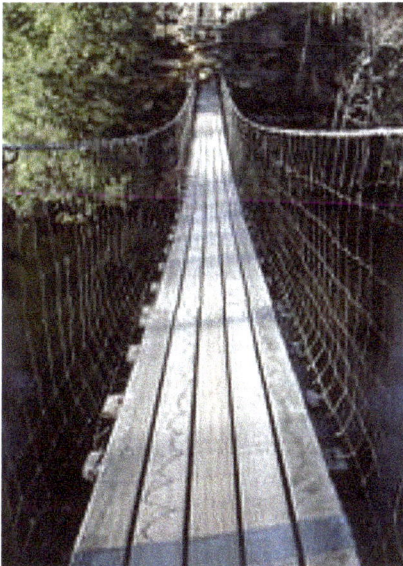

Swinging Bridge at Pleasant Grove Recreation Area

Morel Mushroom in Spring

Willow Grove Receives First "Clean Marina"
Assessment through the Corps of Engineers, 2005.
Congressman Bart Gordon of Tennessee Presents
Flag to Darren Shell

Larry and Sheryl Shell, Thanksgiving, 1982
A Stringer Worthy of Giving Thanks!

Authors Darren and Sheryl
With 35 Pound Catfish, 1985
Nice Tube Socks!

Mitchell Creek During the Freeze of 1977

Livingston Dock (Now Mitchell Creek Marina)
Freeze of 1977

Lake Lover, Jace Stoops of Monticello, Indiana, 2006

Blake Ledbetter   *Lauren Shell and Shaela Ledbetter*

Mill Creek Falls, 2006

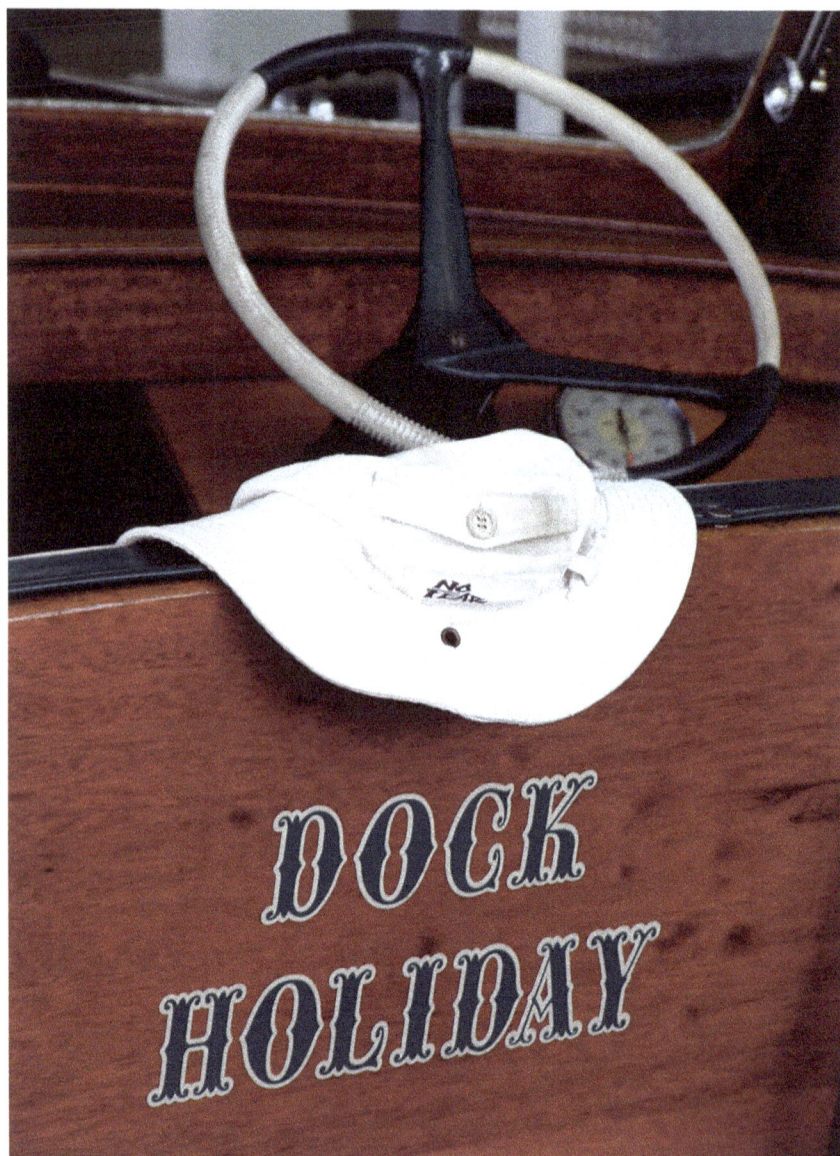

1958 Lyman and the Gravedigger's Day Off Hat

Other Works by the Darren Shell

Fiction

Lost Treasure
The Old Lady of the Lake
Graveyard Tour
Death Wish
Leaflings
Angel's Share
No Safety Bars and Other Stories
Nothing Private
Street Smart

Nonfiction

The Stories from Dale Hollow Lake

A Stone's Throw
(The History of the Game of Marbles in Tennessee and Kentucky)

The Big Ones
(The World Record Smallmouth Bass of Dale Hollow Lake)

The Last Smallmouth (written with Tony Bean)

Against Heavy Odds (The Eddie Swanson Story)

Video

Journey to Old Willow Grove
(A Historical look at Dale Hollow Lake)

www.DarrenShell.com

Buy Darren's books at Amazon.com

About the Authors

Darren Shell works at his family-run marina on Dale Hollow Lake in middle Tennessee. He has written a number of books, both fiction and nonfiction. His stories and lectures about the lake and local history have gained him the title of "Gravedigger" in surrounding communities. Most days you can find him at the marina…if he's not out "digging."

Sheryl Shell is a semi-retired marina owner and mother of two. She lives in Clay County, Tennessee, with her husband, Larry. Her studies of lake history sparked her interest to compile this book.

www.ingramcontent.com/pod-product-compliance
Lightning Source LLC
Chambersburg PA
CBHW041820090426

42811CB00009B/1049